SO WE BELIEVE SO WE PRAY

SO WE BELIEVE SO WE PRAY

George A. Buttrick

ABINGDON PRESS
Nashville

SO WE BELIEVE, SO WE PRAY

Published by Abingdon Press in 1992 as an Abingdon Classic.
Previously published under Library of Congress Catalog Card No.: 51-9467

This book is printed on acid-free recycled paper.

Library of Congress Cataloging-in-Publication Data

BUTTRICK, GEORGE ARTHUR. 1892–
  So we believe, so we pray / George Arthur Buttrick.
  p. cm—(Abingdon classics)
  Includes index.
  ISBN 0-687-39049-4 (alk. paper)
  1. Theology, Doctrinal. 2. Lord's prayer. I. Title. II. Series.
BT75.2.B83   1991
226.9′606—dc20   91-38878

MANUFACTURED IN THE UNITED STATES OF AMERICA

To

SHIRLEY, EDITH, and BETTY

daughters
in law
and
in love

διὰ τὸ ἔχειν με ἐν τῇ καρδίᾳ ὑμᾶς

Foreword

THE YEAR 1992 marks the centennial of George Arthur Buttrick's birth, and it is a fitting tribute to his memory that Abingdon Press is reissuing *So We Believe, So We Pray* in the Abingdon Classics series at this time. And it is a joy and a challenge to add the words of this foreword to the new edition of the book. All who knew him recognized that George Buttrick was a remarkable, exceptional person; one could say he was a genius if that word had not had its true meaning worn out from misuse. His intense mental powers showed clearly in his disciplined concentration; his piercing insights into human nature, society, and Christian faith; and his capacities for listening, seeing, and observation. Those who knew him during his days in New York City at Madison Avenue Presbyterian Church and Union Theological Seminary (the time when *So We Believe, So We Pray* was written) recall above all else his serious disposition and commanding demeanor. Those who knew him some decades later remember his profundity, wit, and charm. And in all times people have spoken of Buttrick's poetic imagination and eloquence, which always stood in contrast to his gravelly voice and idiosyncratic, even eccentric style of preaching and lecturing. One minister, a renowned pulpiteer, who knew George Buttrick only through his published works remarked, "In Dr. Buttrick there is a subtlety, an exquisiteness of mind and language, that reaches the sublime."

To have known George Buttrick personally was pure confirmation of this opinion. Seldom has God brought out of the human race a wiser soul, who in turn was refined by a life of study and devotion. He always seemed to have the right word, and he always knew whether to say it. A grieving widow, overwhelmed with guilt because of the accidental death of her husband, told Buttrick, "I just can't forgive myself." "Dear woman," he replied, "I didn't know *that* was *your* job!" But one winter evening Buttrick and a strongly agnostic acquaintance walked together, and the other man spoke of the pain of life that caused his doubt. The two came upon an upright construction crane with a steel beam hoisted high. Against the setting sun the crane and the beam formed a dark and somber cross. "It's a cruel world," said the acquaintance as he pointed. Buttrick reported that immediately he thought, looking at the same sight, "But it's a redeemed world!'; yet, the line went unspoken, for he said, "It would have been sheer arrogance to have uttered it in that moment." There are times to speak and times to listen, and George Buttrick knew the difference.

The wisdom was clearly a gift, but in large measure Buttrick's understanding was cultivated through much long hard study. Yet, that there was a natural frame upon which the erudition hung was always evident from his delightful sense of humor. In retirement Buttrick occasionally labored as an interim pastor. Once the congregation he served called a young minister straight from seminary to his first charge. Some months passed and, then, one day Buttrick appeared in the young man's office to pay a "check-up" visit. They spoke of the life of the congregation, and as Buttrick seemed ready to leave, he asked, "Bob, are you studying?" "Oh, yes," came the reply. To which Buttrick queried, "How much are you studying?" "At least four hours a week," the young pastor said. "No, Bob, at least four hours per day," declared Buttrick; to which the poor pastor protested, "But, Dr. Buttrick, if I study four hours a day I'll be as smart as you." "Right, Bob," Buttrick answered.

Stories about George Buttrick are legion, and they could go on and on; but the appropriateness of honoring Buttrick by releasing the long-out-of-print *So We Believe, So We Pray* instead of a volume of anecdotes about him should not go unnoticed. Though he was an avid reader of biographies, Buttrick believed the only sure guide to misunderstanding a person was through an autobiography. "No human can ever adequately explain the whole of a human life," he once stated. He even regarded biographies, and especially autobiographies of recognized Christian leaders as a genuine disservice to the life of the Church. "It puts the light in the wrong place, and so distorts the truth." Buttrick was a gold mine of stories, generally about others and rarely about himself. But always, if you listened carefully you found he was moving through the stories toward something or Someone Else. He saw in life more than the viewing of 20/20 vision. Once, however, an eager young admirer pressed him asking, "Dr. Buttrick, how have you managed to accomplish so much?', and Buttrick answered, "Because Jesus Christ is more real to me than I am to myself." He spoke quietly, as a matter of fact, and confidently in faith.

This book is about that faith. Elegant and articulate though it is, *So We Believe, So We Pray* is no easy read. Far from being complex or obscure, Buttrick simply perceives and meditates on the breadth and depth of Christian faith in a far more comprehensive manner than that to which we are accustomed. Yet, the more we know, the more we are aware of what we do not know. Thus, in *So We Believe, So We Pray* Buttrick speaks of the riches of Christian faith, all the while in honest recognition of his human limitations. He never succumbs to the temptation to reduce faith to facts and propositions; still he affirms throughout this book the reality of faith and its foundation. Those who really read this book, who ponder every line—even every word— with the same great care that Buttrick chose and wrote them will find themselves rewarded, even blessed. To travel with George Arthur Buttrick through the living fields of belief and prayer is to walk with an excellent guide who points to the seemingly all too familiar ("the main avowals of Christian faith, and then the petitions of the Lord's Prayer") and, yet, notices and draws our attention to dimensions of our faith we have somehow never before recognized. May all readers walk with Buttrick, as he himself walked, in the grace of our Lord.

Marion L. Soards
Alexander von Humboldt-Haus
Münster (Westfalen), Germany
Erntedankgottesdienst 1991

Contents

SO WE BELIEVE, SO WE PRAY

PART I

So We Believe

CHAPTER I

Born to Believe

> "For the which I also suffer these things: nevertheless I am not ashamed: for I know whom I have believed, and am persuaded that he is able to keep that which I have committed unto him against that day."　　　　　　　　　　　　II Timothy 1:12

A MAGAZINE editor, who has both chance and desire to keep his finger on the public pulse, tells of a comment made by a member of his staff. It was spoken, not as from reporter to editor, but man to man in half confession: "There's a vague change. People want to believe something. But what? They look at the church, then look away again—it is not there. What can a man believe?"

Actually, the change is not in the fact that "people want to believe something," for human nature has always harbored that want. However much people may want to question and know, far more eagerly they want to believe. Faith is as instinctive as breathing; skepticism at long last is an affront. People not only want to believe; they *do* believe—something or someone. If they do not believe in God, they try to believe in success or in themselves. When faith in Christ is thwarted or shelved, faith does not cease; as well might a man resolve not to breathe. No, he then sets his faith on gadgets or Hitler or scientism. Modern man, while repudiating the "sentimentalism" of religious belief, may have sold out to a vast fiction; perhaps he worships his own arguments as the final test of truth. So the "change" indicated by the reporter is not in the fact that "people want to believe something," for that basic want can never change, but in the fact that people are growing tired of modern nostrums and are searching for a better faith.

I

Why do we now desert our belief in "progress" and the cult of power? Nobody can make accurate appraisal—we are too close to the picture—but a provisional answer can be given. Modern man vaguely knows that there is value in selfhood which totalitarianisms do not honor. Free enterprise has not honored it either, for capitalism has stressed acquisitiveness and so invited strife; and therefore the swing to some form of commonalty need not have surprised us. But communism in its German or Russian form virtually erases the individual; he is fodder. For what? For some forthcoming aggregate of individuals. Thus totalitarianisms not only make no sense but are an insult to the soul. Bricks may be used to prop the social structure, but people are not bricks. People are more even than intricate meshings of bone and nerve and brain: they have "value." Modern man does not clearly know what he means by "value"; it is one of the words by which he tries to shut out the mystery of God. But he is dimly aware of resident worth, and knows that it must be kept. He is looking for a faith that will keep it—on a better level than acquisitiveness.

There are other causes of the "vague change." Our materialism has become surfeit to those who have profited, and mistaken envy in those who have been denied the world's dubious "goods." Meanwhile our scientism has left us with arid minds, and has been desecrated to ends of destruction. That latter perversion has hastened the change. For modern men have been obliged to confront a strain of demonism in human nature, an evil that can turn brilliant brain to the manufacture of H-bombs. The demonism may be doom. Does it come from some subliminal unconscious, or is it the work of some devil? It is also guilt, if we regard man as having any responsibility. What to do about demonism and guilt? Is there a structure of grace over against the dark unconscious, a shaft upward as well as a shaft downward? Our modernisms have collapsed, not merely because in some selfish utility "they do not work," but because they leave us bereft in our essential nature. That is why "there is a vague change."

The change was sure to come. People are born to believe. They cannot live on questionings. For a man to say in honesty, "I do not believe that dogma," may be a virtue, provided he can add with radiant mind, "Yet I do believe this . . ." But without some positive avowal his negations become only darkness, for belief is as native as breathing. People cannot live on "facts." Facts are not faith. Of late we have had a windfall of facts, in such multitude that man's mind can hardly count them, let alone comprehend their meaning. This inability is a portent that university education refuses to confront. It raises the whole problem of *essential* curriculum, and makes clear that a windfall of facts can be a famine of faith. Facts are like bricks. Modern man now spends his time analyzing the bricks to make sure they are sound. Thus the house is never built, and the spirit of man is left naked to the storm. Facts cannot supply their own meaning; only faith can give them meaning. A poor faith will give them a low meaning—atomic power will become H-bombs.

Suppose our questionings were all answered (it would be dubious gain!) , a positive faith *on the level of the mind only* would still be forlorn. For such a faith would not be faith. It would hardly be better than a proposition in geometry. "A straight line is the shortest distance between two points," but what of it? It is not food for the spirit. Let no reader construe this comment as a plea for an obscurantist faith. Faith must never be counter to reason; yet it must always go beyond reason, for the nature of man is more than rationalism. Faith is emotion as well as reason. Faith is a valor daring the unknown. This Hitler knew. He rushed in to fill the vacuum made by our scientific negations. His speeches were ranting nonsense, but they had fervor; and if choice must be made between rationality and fervor, men will choose fervor. His cause was nihilism, but at least he provided pageantry and a vow unto death; and if men must choose between a scientific "order of life" on the one hand and nihilism plus banners plus a dangerous commitment on the other, they will choose nihilism. We can learn from our apocalyptic time that men must believe with emotion as well as with brain. Emotion is e-motion: motion out. Emotion is in very fact our motive power. So there is a "vague change." Beyond totalitarianism and capitalism, beyond materialism and demonism, beyond negation and an arid mind, "people want to believe something. But what?"

"They look at the church, then look away again—it is not there." Perhaps that averted glance is just, and perhaps unjust. The Church is compromised, for wherein has it been very different in these latter years from the mass of mankind? The Church, far from fertilizing a worldly desert, has been reduced to a trickle by the surrounding sand. The church in Czarist Russia was thus almost suffocated. The church in Germany failed in any strong and instant protest against Hitler; though, it must be added, the measure of protest that did rise came from the church. The church in America: has it not been dyed in the colors of competitive materialism? Yet the survival of the Church, in view of its timidities and even treacheries, becomes more strange; there must be life at its heart. It has dared tyrannies and cannibal isles, without much benefit of money or prestige, and has printed the sign of the Cross on our planet. Admitting that the Church is largely husk, there must be some heart of living grain. Perhaps if we could find *that,* our "vague change" would have direction and goal.

II

"I know whom I have believed." The word is clear, like the sound of a finely tempered bell. It is sure and decisive; this man, we guess, had cut through his doubts, as sunrise cuts through gloom. Who is he? The modern cliché brands him a dogmatist who fettered the free spirit of Christian faith with chains of coercive theology. That charge is caricature. Paul was a prisoner of his date, as is every man, and so he interpreted his faith in the thought forms of his time and training; and to us these forms seem harsh. Yet he wrote with such pristine light that each succeeding age has been his debtor. His mind is a university—no thinker can ignore him. His statesmanship welded groups of freemen and slaves into a world-wide church. His humanity was so large and warm that friends would walk miles with him rather than leave him, and then weep in very sorrow when the parting could no longer be stayed. His courage is consternation to any weak will. His poetry—"Though I speak with the tongues of men and of angels, and have not love" [1] —has been a sky above man's journeyings. The modern man who patronizes him as a "dogmatist" would be comic, if he were not so deformed.

"I know *whom* I have believed." *Whom* is the arresting word. We ask, as the reporter asked of the editor, "*What* can a man believe?" Paul might answer: "If all you believe is 'what,' belief or disbelief will not greatly matter." We are men of energetic hand, and therefore we have looked for the magic formula or the perfect scheme. We shall never find them, and if we did, they would kindle no flame in us; for men cannot rouse a crusade for atomic power or some economic plan. We are men of mind, and therefore we have looked for a philosophy to answer all our questionings. We shall never find it; and if we did, it would condemn us to live in a cold house. Hannah Arendt takes issue with the religious tradition as follows: "I would really like to know who among the great philosophers since Spinoza and Descartes—outside of Catholic philosophy—accepted 'traditional religious beliefs.'" [2] The petulant conceit in such a statement is hard to miss. Of course there *have* been great Protestant philosophers, but that fact is beside the point. This is the main issue: so long as a man is merely a philosopher, he cannot believe. The world always exceeds his mind, and he himself is more than mind. If he brings to belief no more than his mind, he is no longer a whole person, and fractional men cannot believe. Any worthy faith must enlist mind and hand and heart.

The object of belief is "whom," not "what." Someone may retort that an atheistic artist can live in passionate faith. Yes, but only because unwittingly he regards beauty as a living thing. Dr. N. E. E. Swann argues that we may tear out Mahomet from Mohammedanism, and even Buddha from Buddhism, but that Christ cannot be cut from Christianity.[5] Perhaps he has overproved his case. Perhaps we cannot tear out a Mahomet or a Buddha from his faith. Is not each of those two faiths named after the man? We cannot tear out personal loyalty from any cause, least of all tear out Christ from Christianity. It is a striking affair that communism, while insisting that it is an economic salvation because mankind (it argues) is economically determined, should almost deify Marx and Lenin. Principles never take life except in a person. There would have been no single-tax movement but for some Henry George.

The object of belief is "whom." Men will turn from machines, plans, and platforms whenever the true leader comes; and if no true leader appears, they will follow a false leader rather than a correct creed, provided that leader has guile and glamor. For we are persons, and real faith must enlist the whole man. That is to say, faith must be *personal* faith. Our real need is a leader who is bone of our bone and flesh of our flesh, who has the "common touch" and shares our burdens, *yet* is not disfigured by our sins or stricken by our transience. It is a large order! Does it not crave the incarnation of all that men at their holiest have meant by God?

III

Functional psychology no longer wins favor; man is one, not a loosely knit collection of faculties and powers.

Mind, emotion, and will flow into one personality; we can demark them only as we demark an eddy or a bend in a stream. But, by some necessity of our nature, the demarcation must be made; and it has value if we bear in mind the essential wholeness. Paul believed with his mind, for the "whom" satisfied his intellect. Christ would satisfy our mind, if we would come to Him to learn. The Incarnation is not alien from our physics-philosophy that tells us of every event that it is "contingency," an uprush from the ground of life, for Christian faith has always maintained that Christ is the transcendent and seminal Event. Does someone say that our physics-philosophies will change? Nothing is more sure. But age after age Christ has found a home in each new philosophy wherein it holds truth, and He will not be stranger to the verity in any coming philosophy. Meanwhile, if we mean by mind the acid that eats away the falsities in any culture, does not Christ win the mind? Or if we mean by mind the vision to forecast the future, according as a man follows this path or that path, is there not penetrating light in the mind of Christ? Or if we mean by mind a power to frame a doctrine of man, the world, and God, do not men return to Him age after age from their mistaken "wisdom"?

Paul believed with his emotions also, for Christ kindled in his heart a passionate flame. Not at first, for Christ at first may repel a man of strong feeling. Who is this Leader who rebukes the natural man, takes sharp issue with our cherished customs, yet suffers insensate tyranny with seeming gentleness? It is not strange that Paul at first persecuted the Christian faith as a madness and Christ as an impostor. But Christ cannot be denied, and His gentleness hides an unstayed power. In a movie [4] which shows only His shadow or His cross moving above a crowd, the hint of Him is more trenchant than the actual presence of any other man. The trumpet praise of a Hallelujah Chorus, the poetry in stone of a Rheims Cathedral, the crucifixion scene on a Tintoretto canvas, when they are duly pondered, become an almost unanswerable apologetic. Who is this Man who has so won the heart of all men?

Paul believed also with his will, for Christ won his deeds at bitter cost, and then turned the bitterness into strange joy. Robert Graves, writing of recent notable conversions to the Romanist faith, has this: "I can see no evidence that they have decided to sell all that they have and follow Jesus, which is essential Christianity." [5] Of one convert in particular he adds: "When he turns his bowler-hat into a begging-bowl and carries a palmer's ragged staff instead of a rolled silk-umbrella, I shall be less reluctant to believe in the reported revival." Perhaps Robert Graves has not probed to the deepest "essential," but he has probed. Christ is at odds with our comfortably selfish world; and faith in Him, if it is real, will set a man against the world. But real pondering of Christ has always worked that revolution. It has captured and redeemed the will. "For the which cause I also suffer these things," said Paul—of "things" that would have affrighted any unbeliever. He drew a trail of blood, his own persecuted blood, across the ancient world. He never knew when ambushed death might strike. Again and again he turned his back on "peace" rather than turn his back on Christ. Why? Because Christ had won his will, so that his will gathered strength to reshape a world.

IV

In the next six chapters we are to ask if Christian faith is the answer to the vague hungers of our half-despairing world. In this chapter we have pleaded that men are born to believe, and that all our modern questionings are worth nothing unless they issue in true faith. Skepticism is an untenable outpost in our warfare, because it is against nature. We have tried to show that men always do believe, finely or falsely, and that all belief is at last personal trust. The proper question is not "What can a man believe?" No "what" can enlist our whole self. The proper question is "Whom can a man believe?" We have therefore drawn a picture of a man who believed in Christ, thus suggesting provisionally that Christ is the answer. Bengel pointed out, in almost his dying word, that Paul would not "let even a preposition come between himself and his Lord." [6] Paul said not "in whom" or "by whom" or "for whom," but "I know whom I have believed." Madame Guyon's last will and testament shows a real faith: "This is my last will and testament . . . It is to Thee, O Lord God! that I owe all things . . . To Thee, in an act of irrevocable donation, I give up both my body

and my soul, to be disposed according to Thy will." [1]
Faith is that kind of commitment, not counter to reason,
but beyond reason in the dangerous venture of love.

The ebb tide of doubt has turned, even though the
incoming tide of faith does not yet strongly flow. People
cannot live by questionings. To keep on saying, "Is this
true?" is like saying endlessly, "Is this food?"—a man
would starve. The questionings are right for only so long;
then a man must venture. A set of principles (*"What* can
a man believe?"*) may interest the mind, but can never
fire the emotions or nerve the will. Our wars are the lurid
symbol of the lack of faith. They cannot save us. Perhaps
they can blast away the dragons, but even so they have
the wretched knack of sowing dragons' teeth. Our gadgets
cannot save us: we despise "savages" who bow to idols,
and then ourselves fall prostrate before radar and production lines. Governmental edicts cannot save us: they
are more likely to be the foolish word of men who have
been corrupted by power. All this we begin to learn:
"There's a vague change."

Paul is a representative Christian. He claimed to
"know"; we shall examine the claim. His faith was not
"what," but "whom"; we shall stand again before the
portrait of Christ and ask if He has ultimacy for faith.
Paul's confidence is a brave and radiant affair: he was
"persuaded that he is able to keep that which I have
committed unto him against that day." What had Paul
"committed"? All that modern man deems "value" in
himself and in the new world for which he yearns.

Against what "day"? Any day—the day when Paul died in lonely martyrdom, the day when the atomic bomb may fall, the first day after death, the drab day when men must walk uncertainly in an uncertain earth. An announcement in hotel rooms reads: "The management provides a safe for valuables." Life is only "Grand Hotel." The interlopers called Pain, Doubt, and Death prowl the corridors. Guests inadvertently leave doors unlocked. The hotel is not fireproof. There is no assurance in the corridors of time, and all man's defenses are vain. His best wit leaves him still exposed to robbery. But The Management has provided a safe, not for any selfishness, but for soul. So the guests can live in a brave gaiety— because of Christ. "I know *whom* I have believed."

CHAPTER II

Faith in God

"Let not your hearts be troubled; believe in God."
John 14:1 R.S.V.

A PROFESSOR of philosophy gave his students this assignment: Show that the traditional proofs for God, the argument from design, the argument from purpose, and all the others, are invalid in logic. I do not know the professor's motives. If he was intent to teach rigorous thinking, he may have been justified. If he was trying to score at the expense of religion, he could have saved time and trouble; for modern seminaries admit without serious misgiving that these time-honored proofs, such as that involving the analogy of Paley's watch,[1] hide fallacies in logic. Somewhere in the argument God is slipped in rather than proved. If any reader is interested to play detective in this issue, he may find the sleuthing shrewdly done in such a book as Douglas Clyde Macintosh's *Theology as an Empirical Science*.[2] But a much more vital interest will ask where God came from that He might be slipped in! He always slips in, and perhaps that fact is itself a better proof than the proofs. The man who says,

"I deny God's existence," has still used the word and presumably knows what it means. Perhaps God is the inescapable axiom of human life: "In Him we live, and move, and have our being." [3]

Soon after Pearl Harbor, when a popular magazine printed news of a revival of religion in the army, a subscriber appropriately named Voltaire H. Zizka wrote a letter branding the article as "lying and hypocrisy":

> You refer to the certainty that God is watching over our soldiers. Did He watch when the Japs slaughtered them while going to church on a memorable Sunday at Pearl Harbor? . . . Where was He when Lidice was wiped off the map? . . . Only with a realistic, sane, atheistic approach will the world of the future be better. Theism and deism have failed. A war bond will do more good than a prayer. [4]

But God slips in even into such a letter. For its atheism is self-contradictory: atheism caused Pearl Harbor and therefore can never cure it. Besides, the author plainly means by "realistic and sane" a resolve on what is honorable, and he implies that such honor has sanction over mankind. God, though the correspondent would not use the name, was in his fervent protest against Lidice; a needs-must commanded him. So perhaps God always slips in, and perhaps that fact is the saving mystery of our pilgrimage.

I

Edwin Arlington Robinson has a word for our time: "The world is . . . a kind of spiritual kindergarten, where millions of bewildered infants are trying to spell God with the wrong blocks." [5] God cannot be spelled in blocks of logic, for God is not a theorem to be proved; and if He were, He would hardly be worth the proving. God cannot be spelled with blocks of science, for God is not mainly an object to be studied; and if He were, the studying could bring no genuine life. Perhaps the proper answer to the doctor who declared, according to a current story,[6] that he had examined the human body and could find no trace of soul is this: "When you are dead and they examine you, they will find no trace of the passion for medical research." Anyone content merely to examine a violin scientifically would never find Bach's "Air for the G String."

Assuming that God is and that He is truly Godlike, it is safe to assume that He will be best known by a venture of friendship. Logic and science will have their place, but hardly more proportionately than in human friendship. The trustworthiness of a next-door neighbor is not demonstrated by a test tube. A man does not propose to a girl scientifically—or if he does, she will be wise to refuse him on the spot. Indeed if God is God, no man will find God; he will be found of God. The initiatives originally and constitutionally belong to God, and only the responses belong to man. Always man has fashioned names for the Mystery. The Chinese Tien means Heaven, the Persian Ahura-Mazda means The Wise Creator, the Egyptian Amon means The Hidden, the Arabic Allah means The Great Adored; and our word God, which stands comparison with any other name, means The Good. God is "the Nameless of the hundred names," [7] a fact that implies that He has found us in a hundred ways. We respond in a name:

Speak to Him thou for He hears, and Spirit with Spirit can meet—
Closer is He than breathing, and nearer than hands and feet. [8]

God will be found, not by our seeking, but by a response in prayer and life to One of whom we are dimly aware—as a child, half waking, responds to the mother who bends over him.

II

So this chapter cannot "prove" God, and would not try. If God is, we shall not escape Him. The best proof is in the fact that He always slips in because we cannot lock the door against Him. All any man can say about God is, "Thus and thus have I seen Him, in an awe that no thing or man could ever quicken." If his hearer should answer, "I do not see," the honesty of the reply should not be questioned. But, fortunately for any discussion of God, every man has seen the Light, even though some men may afterward doubt their inward eyes; and every man has heard the Footfall, though some men may afterward wonder if the sound was real. What are the signs of His presence?

The world about us seems to bear His signature. New universes become commonplace as our telescopes increase in power. They are sextillions of miles away, a sextillion being represented by a one and twenty-one zeros. They are so distant that light, traveling at 186,000 miles per second, takes a billion years to reach us. They hold stars, such as Mira, so large that a train starting its journey at the birth of Christ and running round the star at forty-five miles an hour would not yet have completed its journey.[9] We speak of skyscrapers, but by comparison with the sky our tallest buildings do not rise tissue-thickness from the ground.

This grandeur of creation is not just power, but miraculously co-ordinated power. My church janitor in Vermont, watching me wrestling clumsily with a block of scrap marble found in my garden soil, remarked with Vermont dryness: "You don't move them things by main force and ignorance." There is no such clumsiness in the creation. The planet while it spins sweeps in an arc round the sun, which itself moves meanwhile on its own mysterious course through space; yet the whole process, terrible in power, is so delicately balanced and safe that children laugh while they scamper. Yes, children also die, and no mortal mind can understand how that dissonance belongs in the symphony. But no one can thoughtfully deny an apparent plan in creation; eyes and light are in precise mutuality; mind and world fit as snugly as the words and melody of a song.

There is beauty about us, more sensitive in design than a Chinese painting. Watch a man working on a beehive. Possibly he wears no gloves—bees are not cruel unless they are threatened. They are a kingdom of exact laws and diversified service. They are lovely in color, the flowers they haunt are lovelier, and between bee and flower there is exact affinity. So we see in the encompassing world power on power, co-ordinated power, power wrought in surpassing beauty. It is hardly possible not to use such words as purpose, or to deny that such words imply personal will. It would not be logical to claim that God may be deduced from contemplation of His world. But who has not felt, however fitfully, that He is *mediated* by His world?

> Whose dwelling is the light of setting suns,
> And the round ocean and the living air,
> And the blue sky, and in the mind of man.[10]

There is an apparent sadism in nature, a fact we shall not ignore. But the Signature remains. Most of the time it may be dim, but for everyman at some luminous moment it is written in shining clarity.

III

The world of humankind bears His countersign. By what deep wisdom are we able to speak of time and eternity? We say that "time flies" and that "civilizations pass," but we could not so speak without some eternal fixity in us by which we mark and measure the flowing of the stream. It is a *holy* fixity, or crime and cruelty would not trouble us. Maurice B. Reckitt has written: "War is not an accident of our civilization: it is but a natural outcome of it." [11] We did not deliberately intend war; even Hitler would have preferred an easier way to empire. We intended a high standard of living and protective tariffs—which perhaps meant the safeguarding of our comfort by causing unemployment in poorer lands. We intended to build airplanes, without much thought of the soul that alone could guarantee their rightful use. We intended to defend our bodies. But we did not intend war. Then who did intend it? It will not avail us to speak merely of some "moral law" interposed between an inactive God and a helpless man. That would be like blaming electrocution on the wires. Men are troubled in conscience about war. They hate its desolations. They are miserable under its threats. They rightly blame humankind for its recurrence. But they also know that they are in the hands of One who would rather see our pride shattered, our homes darkened and our cities blitzed than that we should lose our souls. All attempts to dissolve the identity of conscience fail at last. It grows? Yes. We see it in different stages in different lands? Yes. It can be mistaken, and even falsely identified with custom and prejudice? Yes. But it breaks through custom to our pain, and always at last it comes as a higher against a lower, however we may try by rationalization to evade its claim. That is why we know that war is the outcome of our civilization. Surely we may say with conviction that Holiness speaks through conscience.

Humankind has gentler movements. Or should we say that *compassion* comes of conscience? The research doctor, seeking a cure for leukemia, does not work for money or fame. His goal is not merely the right medical prescription. The truth is that he cannot bear the sight of people dying helplessly; his thought is on them more than on the disease. But why? Why should anyone worry about other people's worries? Yet everywhere, in settlement houses and hospitals, in churches and homes, there are people who gratuitously carry their neighbors' burdens and could not easily tell why. Compassion commands us. When we try to command it or limit it, our systems go to wreck. Who keeps alive compassion in our race? The fact that tyrannies have again and again bedeviled us makes more strange the "survival value" of love. Pain leaves kindness harder to explain. The woman who looked at the vastness of ocean for the first time and asked, "Who keeps filling it up?" had the right question. Who keeps filling up the ocean of idealism? When millions live for the main chance, why have there always been saints and martyrs?

> Martyrs! who left for our reaping
> Truths you had sown in your blood.[12]

Conscience and compassion in men surely have a source beyond mankind, for man is but a creature. This is a guess? Call it rather "the soul's invincible surmise." [13]

Moreover, *Jesus* is within our humankind. We shall plead that He is also from beyond humankind, and that He is always above us. But, however that may be, He was "found in fashion as a man." [14] He took on himself our

35

nature. He is inextricably in the fabric of human history.
How shall He be explained? If the deviltries that disfigure
our life are an enigma of darkness, He is more persistently
an enigma of light. For we can measurably interpret darkness by Him (He redeemed darkness by His Cross and
still abides) , whereas we can never interpret Him by any
darkness. If we see red in a runnel as it crosses a sandy
beach, we say: "There is iron hidden in the hills." If we
see Christ in the midst of human life, shall we not say:
"There is Christlikeness at the wellspring of our days"?
These issues belong for discussion in the next chapter,
but here and now we must remember Him as we try to
trace the signature of God. Surely the sign is clear in Him.
Surely He stands apart from any merely human scrib-
bling. The artist Haydon, in his picture of the Triumphal
Entry, succeeded well with human faces, for there he used
his friends as models for the friends of Jesus. Keats and
Wordsworth are among them in excellent portraiture.
But with the face of Jesus the artist was at a loss. Eight
times he tried, and seven times painted out the failure.
The eighth attempt remains, but only as a broken hint of
a transcendence that no man can portray. The donkey on
which Christ rides is drawn convincingly, so that one
critic said mockingly: "Your ass is the Saviour of your picture." [15] But we should pity Haydon, for who could depict
Christ? That question is its own argument, better than
any logical proof. "The Word became flesh and dwelt
among us." [16]

IV

Perhaps our discussion is open to the charge that we have taken only shining instances. So let us grasp the nettle. It is a dark jungle rather than nettle, and it grows across every man's path. What of tragedy and seemingly senseless pain? Mark this striking fact: in times of widespread suffering our race does not rebel against God or deny Him as much as at other times, but rather turns to pray. C. S. Lewis rightly contends that only one fact in human experience is more universal and stubborn than the fact of pain, namely, the fact of the sense of God; and that therefore we must explain not only pain but primarily men's faith in God.[17] He could have gone further: the two facts are strangely linked.

Honesty compels the confession that whole reaches of pain are chargeable to our abuse of freedom, a freedom without which nevertheless we could not be men. Many an automobile accident comes of selfish driving, and many a tenement fire has been caused by a tenant's carelessness with matches and a landlord's greedy refusal to change a firetrap into a fireproof home. We cannot be less than grateful for our freedom; we cannot blame God if we profane it. Honesty obliges another admission: darkness in our world can be the womb of light. Perhaps we should not say that pain *causes* valor and faithfulness, but at least pain *occasions* this nobleness. *Speaking of Operations* [18] is a hilarious book and serves the by-purpose of warning us from a topic that makes for boredom. But why do people like to talk of their operation? They faced a

37

crisis in reasonably brave resolve. They came through, and are now veterans casually discussing their wars before the raw recruits. They learned a truth that comfort could not teach. They gained selfhood and are therefore under greater temptation to talk about themselves. Most men would admit that access of soul has come, not from the bright and carefree years, but from pain-filled stretches of the road. Man's music, like Debussy's, is wrung from loneliness and seeming failure.

In the paragraph above, two vast issues, man's freedom to cause pain and pain's doorway to grace, have been scantily treated and almost summarily dismissed. Why the short shrift? Because when tragedy comes, it would be near insult to remind the sufferer that much pain comes of

the rarity
Of Christian charity
Under the sun,[19]

and perhaps worse insult to propose that he can now grow in soul. In any event, God is behind the gift of man's freedom with all its potential explosiveness; and God is behind war's penalty of desolation. Would He be God if His last word were: "You abused your freedom, and now you must take the consequence"? Would He be God if character must be grown by wars, if His "harvest-fields" must "be dunged with rotten death"? [20]

There are deeper facts than any discussion of man's freedom or of a possible access of soul in pain. There are deeper facts even than the strange fact that men *seek* pain, braving oceans and sky and the hazardous cause, as if life did not bring enough pain of itself. The deepest fact is this: when tragedy comes, we know that another Will has cut across our will. Perhaps that conviction always comes first, even before the bitter protest and rebellion. An engine explodes on a small boat, a dearly loved body is taken from the lake. The first thought is, at least for me: "Eternity has dealings with us—in a paradox of terror and love." Then comes the rebellion: "Why? This is senseless!" But even the rebellion hints another Will, for no man could rebel against an engine or a lake. Tragedy is thus apocalypse—of a Mystery. That is why tragedy is more likely to drive us to God in faith than to alienate us. Tragedy is catharsis because it is apocalypse. Tragedy leads us to say with Bagehot that we live "on the very edge of two dissimilar worlds; on the very line on which the infinite, unfathomable sea surges up, and just where the queer little bay of this world ends." He adds in the same deep wisdom: "We count the pebbles on the shore, and image to ourselves as best we may the secrets of the great deep." [21] Tragedy lifts our eyes to the mysterious Sea, from which both the "fear of the Lord" [22] and His salvation come to us. Tragedy is itself the signature of God, whose ways are "past finding out." [23]

V

Has this chapter "proved" God? With all its share of human folly, it would not try. To attempt a demonstration of God would be presumption carried to the edge of blasphemy. All any man can do in this issue is to say: "Here and here as I have journeyed an awe-struck silence has fallen on me, and I have felt God." There are many ways of knowing. A man can know the stock-market quotations, and he can know architecture, and he can know his friend. The three knowings are in three different realms. If God is God, the best knowledge of God must come through a higher kind of friendship. So the "proof" is in a venture: we dare to live as in the presence of the Unseen Companion who ever and again takes us unawares. Robert Bridges has said that God seems at times no more than the reflection of a man's own face in the window as he peers vainly into a darkened house.[24] That is true, just as it is true that at other times God seems like a friend's smile and a welcoming fireside seen through that same window. In any event it would do the man little good to keep gazing at his own reflection. Were the man to kneel down in the cottage and pray, "Lord, Thy will be done, that I may live in gay soul and valorous faith"; and were he then to stride through the rain to help a neighbor because the sometimes-seen goodness of God requires it, God would become for him not shadow but the very substance of life.

So faith, while it never affronts reason, always goes beyond reason in brave venture. It prays. That is why this book links a discussion of the main Christian affirmations with a discussion of the Lord's Prayer. It worships, casting itself adoringly on the "black daylight" of the Mystery. It walks the daily road saying, "In truth He is near even

though unseen," and lives in response to the Presence.
For if God is God, He cannot force Himself on us, or rant
from the sky, or blind us with excess of light. If God is
God, the quiet road through Bethlehem must be the way
of His best journeyings. For our sake He will

> Hold us secure behind the gates
> Of saving flesh and bone,[25]

lest we be overwhelmed by His glory; and for His love's
sake He will walk with us the common ways of earth, if
we will trust. Such a faith proves itself in life. We have
recently put atheism to the test. In Russia it has been
avowed; in America it has been widespread, though var-
nished with religion. We see atheism in its poisonous
fruits, just as we see in some Paul or Francis the healing
leaves and life-giving fruits of faith.

VI

It is tragic that we should still be trying to spell God
with the wrong blocks. Argument cannot find Him, for
He is not a proposition to be proved. Science has its place,
but in the kitchen, not in the living room; and science
cannot of itself find God, because God is not a formula to
be discovered or a thing to be studied. Faith never requires a man to disown his intelligence; if faith should
make that demand, faith would cease to be faith and become mere superstition. But faith goes beyond the mind.
It is personal trust. It obeys conscience, if need be like a
sailor tacking against the wind amid the compromising

crosscurrents of our world, but keeping the goal of Christ always in mind. It lives in good will and kindliness, grasping the other man's nettle of pain, thus to find that the sting is gone from its own nettle. It walks the way of prayer, which only childlike trust can walk. Thus it finds the promise fulfilled: "Then shall we know, if we follow on to know the Lord." [26]

Chaucer counsels: "Hold the highroad, thy spirit guiding thee." [27] We are led by Someone stronger and holier than our own spirit, else our poorer self would break us. The venture of trust finds another Hand in the darkness: He leads us. But "Hold the highroad" is still sound wisdom. The road of self-asserting power leads to Rome, and to its "decline and fall." The busy road of acquisitive trade leads to—name your own city, with its cavernous streets echoing to a cacophony of driven footsteps. The "highroad" led in Chaucer's day to Canterbury, with its altar where men worshiped and thus learned to love. But the soul's "highroad" leads beyond any Canterbury, to a City "not made with hands, eternal in the heavens." [28] Hold the highroad of ventured trust, and let God lead you.

CHAPTER III

Faith in Jesus Christ

"And Philip said, If thou believest with all thine
heart . . . And he answered and said, I believe that
Jesus Christ is the Son of God."   Acts 8:37

ARTHUR BALFOUR, philosopher and one-time
premier of Great Britain, was lecturing after the First
World War, it is said, on pathways to a new world. The
meeting, if reading memory is right, was held in the
hall of Edinburgh University. He pleaded for knowledge
in world affairs, for training in statecraft, and for what he
vaguely called "morality." Just as he finished, a Chinese
student rose to ask in a voice that all could hear, "But, sir,
what about Jesus Christ?" [1]

There seemed no *place* then for Jesus Christ. Evolution was a magic word, and how could Jesus fit into the
ascent of evolution? If He was perfect, as the churches
claimed, He should have come, not in midmost of the
process, but as its climax. However, men have had
long thoughts about evolution. It is not an unstoppable
escalator even in the animal realm; there are locked types,
and reversions to type. Besides, we now know that each
new event *is* new and cannot be explained *in toto* by its

43

antecedents. Contingency, not evolution, is now the magic word, until some new word arrives. Besides, even if every claim for evolution were granted, man has some freedom and can therefore be the wrecker of his evolution; and so presumably he needs both a power within and a goal beyond, such as—Jesus. But there seemed no place then for Jesus. Men believed in an unbreakable chain of cause and effect, and a heavenly being in such a chain was an incongruity that no intelligent man could accept. Now we know that any rigid doctrine of cause and effect is outmoded, and perhaps exploded, because in each new event there is a veritable and unpredictable newness. Someday we may learn from our blunders: instead of judging Jesus by each new theory, we shall judge each new theory by Him.

In those days, when the Chinese student asked his startling question, there seemed to be no *need* for Christ. We were getting along very well by ourselves, thank you. We had a lien on the future. In military parlance, the situation was well in hand. The university was conquering all ignorance: we ignored the fact that every mystery solved rouses six other mysteries from sleep, and that man never knows what a day of life, still less the day of death, will bring. The hospital was curing all disease: we forgot the little matter of our nerves and of our nihilism. Psychiatry would forgive all our sins, which we regarded only as frustrations: we forgot that a guilt complex is guilt as well as complex, and that guilt may be beyond man's power. There had been a war unfortunately, but that was due to the Kaiser's megalomania: we had not realized yet that there was a virus in the blood of mankind. We were ignorant not only about Jesus but also about our own nature. We had not yet confronted the fact of demonism in us. We still clung to the notion that man is an incipient angel. So when that youth asked, "But, sir, what about Jesus Christ?" the distinguished audience probably pitied him and deplored his interruption. But now, when science becomes doom, when wars that were to free us from fear have become worse wars breeding worse fears, "what about Jesus Christ?" Our knowledge and morality cannot save us. What about *His* power to save?

I

From one point of view Jesus is painfully human. Painfully is the exact word—He shared our pains. At first blush He seems to be locked in our dilemma rather than sovereign over it. He went to the synagogue school like any neighbor's child. He worked at a bench, with weariness in his muscles like our weariness, with blood in His veins like our blood. Deceitful men gypped Him. Careless men forgot to pay Him for His work. He was caught in the crosscurrents of His time, for His land felt the impact of world affairs. He met traders from far lands. Perhaps He spoke the *koine* Greek, which was widely spoken from Spain to northern India, as well as His native Aramaic. Besides, He lived in an "occupied" land; He had to decide, like any Jewish man of His generation, if He should join the open insurrection against Roman tyranny, or work with the underground, or walk some "idealistic" road. Nothing could be more mistaken than the phrase sometimes used of His life, "the Syrian Idyll" —His days were no idyll. Lord Morley's description, "the sublime mystic of the Galilean hills," [2] is similarly erroneous—He was no dreamy "mystic" or celestially remote, or we would not so sharply debate Him. Life for Him was as hard as the nails in His shop, or the nails in His Cross.

He taught, even though His enemies were right when they claimed that He was not versed in the schools. He did not evade then-current issues, as witness the day when He spoke of the local tragedy of a falling tower. He did not peddle vague "principles"; His truth was through the matter in hand. He cut across shams and greeds, yet never failed in love. He did not join the insurrection or the underground, but chose another course. He ran foul of Barabbas and the "revolt," and would today. He ran foul of the religious community, and would today, except for the saving heart of lowly devotion that always lives within the Church; for He was branded a heretic, though worship was the flame of His life. He ran foul of the empire, and would today; empire, together with the vested interests of the Temple traders and the Temple authorities, slew Him —not because He was a serious threat in their eyes, but because He was a troublemaker and because empires do not long tolerate troublemakers. He was strung up, and that was that. Could any story be more painfully human? Whatever other titles we claim for Him, He was "bone of our bone, and flesh of our flesh." [3]

We must pause to notice that any savior of men, on whatever level, must share the common life. We may find that Jesus is and must be "from above," but that fact cannot cancel the requirement that he must dwell among us in our very nature. A visiting seraph would be an insult. We might ask him bitterly, "Come slumming?" An angel masquerading as a man hardly belongs on Forty-second Street or in bombed Hiroshima. Is there not a story of a composer who was asked to write a national anthem for some distant land, and who rightly replied in dismay, "But I do not live there"? Jesus could have composed no music for our world—it is now deathless music—if He had not lived among us through birth and death. So the fact that He was painfully human is a prime and necessary fact.

II

Then "what about Jesus Christ?" The word Christ, *Christos,* is the Greek word for Messiah. Modern New Testament scholarship believes that He did not claim the title, except by indirection; but He has won it. Perhaps He refrained from explicit claim (unless indeed He broke through that self-confinement when He answered Pilate's question) [4] because He could not accept the earthy and nationalistic meanings which were attached to the title in His day; perhaps He refrained from very lowliness of soul. But He is now Messiah for millions of more-or-less devoted followers. He has won also the title *Kurios* or Lord. That title was the familiar word "master" as used by slaves of their overlord; but even in that day it had sovereign overtones in religious speech, and in the early church it was used as men use it when they worship God. He has won also the title *Logos* or the Word, a name that means the thrust of God's creative wisdom. To pretend that the titles were bestowed as part of a devious plot is nonsense. Men done to death in the Roman arena for their faith were not devious, or earthily inclined to plot their own cruel death. To pretend that they were guilty of self-hypnotism is no smaller folly: had you been seeking realistic honesty of love in those days, you would have found it best in the Church. The fact is that His followers when He died were plunged not only into grief but into dismay, for a cross was then reckoned a curse. The Church did not lift Him from His niche; manifestly He lifted the Church. Then "what about Jesus Christ?" There are mysteries in Him that our casual age has ignored.

He is the Universal Man. On my shelves there are about one hundred lives of Christ, a mere fraction of those that have been published. The authors represent almost as many points of view. Among them are a Russian essayist, an Italian novelist, a Wisconsin poet, an English progressive, and a French theologian.[5] One book, entitled *Each with His Own Brush*,[6] gives pictures of Christ from many lands. In those from Africa, Christ is an African native; in the Chinese Nativity pictures the Babe has tiny upraised slits for eyes. There is a statue of Him on a ridge of the high Andes between Chile and Argentina, though

He Himself was born and lived in what we now call Palestine.[6] No other leader has thus won the instinctive devotion of the race. Confucius is Chinese, Buddha is Indian, but Christ belongs to mankind. This is a portent: He is "the Son of man." Admittedly He causes controversy and conflict, but that should be expected; recoil is always light's first effect on clay-shuttered eyes. But who else has so captured the heart of man in every land? It is said that the king of England, visiting a military hospital, took one patient completely by surprise; but the soldier rallied strongly, offered his hand, and said: "Put it there, sir, I've heard of you." Wherever Christ has gone, people have heard of Him in a much deeper hearing—in some need and longing of the soul. A universal Man is a *sine qua non,* in world government for an instance; for, though world government must come in some form if our world is to remain, it can never come unless at its heart there is more than a cold schema of government. For man must love before he can be loyal. Thus only a universal Man can win real unity in our world. Let the reader follow the implications of the universality of Jesus: He will thus explore a new Canaan.

He is the Worshiped Man. It is too late in the day to deny that people are born to worship. When true worship decays, worship is not disavowed; a perverted worship erects a pagan altar. There is a primal awe in us, and the lowly Jesus has drawn it to Himself. We are baptized, married, and buried in His name. This fact is such a commonplace that we no longer scrutinize it. But why should we turn in the crises of life to a Detroit mechanic—or a Galilean Carpenter? He has divided the calendar into before and after, so that even modern Russia must date its statecraft by His birth. Again we do not ask why, though our reckoning of time from the first Christmas is a staggering portent. It is far more than deference to a leader, such as that which reckoned Roman calendars from the birth of Augustus; for Jesus by the standards of His time was not a leader but a man obscure in life and cursed in death. That Jesus has set the year 1 means that our world has been apprehended by Him at the point of awe; He is the *Mysterium Tremendum*. It means furthermore that, wittingly or unwittingly, we accept His philosophy of time; all ages before Him lead up to Him, all ages after Him are in His light and power. Is He not the worshiped Man? He overwhelmed the ancient Sabbath in a new Sunday. Our finest architecture, music, and art are offered to Him in adoration. Does someone say, "Not by many millions in the earth"? No. Some have never heard His music; some have heard it only as it is played out of tune by occidental pride and power; and some refuse to expose themselves to its wonder. But these facts do not disprove Him; our selfishness is never His crime. Meanwhile there are multitudes who bow at His Name and other multitudes who say in secret: "Of course He is the answer."

He is the Forgiving Man. We are striking off vast issues in small paragraphs, so that the portrait—if any man could ever draw it!—etched sparingly may have a sharper clarity. Jesus forgave sins. We do not question His right

50

but rather are brought to tears. These facts mean much more than that we count Him worthy to forgive. Such worthiness, if it were all, would still be a spiritual miracle. We search the record of His life and, like Pilate, we can "find no fault" [7] in Him. Some have pointed to a flaw, or what they thought was flaw, but His life has risen in its own instant answer; and mankind at large, age on age, surely under the impact of the Spirit, has known that He alone lived without any shadowed memories. Sinlessness is too thin a word; His holy compassion was not a negative scruple, not abstinence only, but a positive passion, a steady flame of love towards God and man. But more is implied in His forgiveness than this white vigil. For, in a certain profound sense, only God can forgive. When we lie, we do more than hurt ourselves, though it is true that the lie breeds inward chaos; and we do more than hurt our neighbor, though it is true that the lie breeds social chaos because it destroys social trust. When we lie, "we break truth." It is our own phrase, and it is accurate; there is a Sanction beyond man, and a lie is a cosmic vandalism, an ultimate disobedience. Thus only Truth, or God, can forgive. Perhaps we must add that we shall not be sure of pardon until Truth takes flesh, walks down our street, knocks on our door, and says, "Thy sins be forgiven thee." That is what Jesus Christ did say. The Pharisees touched a nerve when, hearing Him pronounce forgiveness of sins, they accused Him of blasphemy. They knew, as every man subtly knows, that only God can forgive. You or I cannot wave a pardoning hand over Sing

Sing or say, "Thy sins be forgiven thee." Then *was* Jesus a blasphemer? Or is God in Him? This prodigious issue of forgiveness rightly demands its own chapter. Here we do no more than look wonderingly at His claim and gift to pardon. It is a "plus" in Him that carries us for beyond human bounds.

He is the Abiding Man. The malice of His foes tried to assure His eclipse in shame. The malice succeeded temporarily with His followers, for they scattered in despair. Three days later an event befell, which, "according to my gospel," [8] is pivotal in human story. His followers cast away despair and donned a hope that no persecution or martyrdom could affright. The Church rose like a phoenix bird from ashes. The New Testament was written, not only without any in-memoriam line, but a-tiptoe with certitude and joy. The critics have spoken of "illusion." They have even proposed that bemused religionists used Him, a dead rabbi, to found a new mystery cult. There are moods when a man could almost wish the "illusion" theory might be true, for the resurrection of Jesus plays havoc with our tidy scientisms and ordered selfishness. It is like light suddenly flashing into Plato's cave.[9] It tells us that we can no longer live in a cavern of half shadows but must learn to walk in an unexplored eternity. But the "illusion" theory actually offers no comfort to our earthiness, for it has no foothold in truth. Can anyone seriously believe it? Does illusion explain the early church with its demand that men shall speak "the truth in love," [10] with its costly honor in a corrupt world, with its valor to die and its power to sing as it died, with its passionate secret even to this day? To confront such a daybreak with the word "illusion" is worse folly than if a man should confront Niagara Falls with the theory that someone must have left the faucet running. Consider the hymn "Fairest Lord Jesus":

> Fair are the meadows,
> Fairer still the woodlands,
> Robed in the blooming garb of spring:
> Jesus is fairer,
> Jesus is purer,
> Who makes the woeful heart to sing.[11]

Try to substitute any other name. Do not plead that the hymn is sentimentalism. It is devotion in very fact, but cauterizing devotion. Religion can become selfish, but for every man who goes to church to coddle his soul, there are two who stay away because Christ's light is pain to selfish eyes. The fact cannot be side-stepped: Jesus is the Abiding Man.

III

Has this chapter "proved" Christ? Books cannot prove Him. Only a brave and loving venture of faith can prove Him. Perhaps we should say that God never provides a "sure thing," if the reader will not misconstrue the phrase. In our real though limited freedom we can always deny Christ, and find a plausible reason for the denial. But there is enough evidence, if evidence is the right word (it savors too much of the police court or the laboratory) , for our belief that the painfully and radiantly human Jesus is yet Deity. That is to say, there is enough evidence to win our venture of faith, but never so much evidence that we are spared the venture. If we were compelled to believe, by very blindingness of light, faith would manifestly cease to be faith; it would be compulsion. A man standing on the banks of the Hudson River at Yonkers must say at a certain hour: "This river flows to the sea." But a few hours later, as he sees the river moving in the other direction, he is obliged to make another judgment: "The ocean has come in upon us."

That double judgment is the confession of the great creeds concerning Christ. Assuredly it is my own witness. His life seen from one point of view is human: He was "found in fashion as a man." [12] Seen from another point of view, as we contemplate His universality, His winning of man's worship, His claim and gift to pardon, His abidingness, we must exclaim: "The ocean of God is come in upon us." We give Him human names such as wisest teacher and noblest prophet, but they are too porous and ridiculously small. They try to compass ocean in a net. Only one word is large enough, the largest word of all: not "divine," for that is an adjective and Christ surpasses every adjective, but—Deity. He is Man, as God gives Manhood for man's aspiring; He is God, as man longs for God and is found of God. All words to describe Him are poor, but some words measurably succeed. These words win my assent in adoration: "God of God, Light of Light, Very God of very God . . . Who for us men and for our salvation came down from heaven, . . . and was made man." [13]

But no creed spares us the venture. We know what that venture means in racial comradeship, in motives of trade, in our warring madness, in respect of prayer. The venture is not easy. It finds no completion on earth. It is often blocked by earth's relativities. But it must not be surrendered. Those who try to follow, stumble; as they stumble, they pray; as they pray, they are forgiven; as they are forgiven, they rise and walk again with a Strength not their own; then as they follow, they "follow on to know the Lord." [14] The lad was right to ask of Balfour: "But, sir, what about Jesus Christ?" It is the only question. For the real issue does not concern the Church, though that question arises in its course. The real issue does not concern a creed, though that also cannot be evaded. The real issue is one of personal loyalty: "But, sir, what about Jesus Christ?" That is the one question, and He is the one answer.

CHAPTER IV

Faith in the Holy Spirit

"He said unto them, Have ye received the Holy Ghost since ye believed? And they said unto him, We have not so much as heard whether there be any Holy Ghost."   Acts 19:2

THIS FAITH IS A chasm before many honest seekers, and the frequent abuse of the doctrine within the Church has widened the breach. Some years ago a group of Christian missionaries sailed for China with no knowledge of the language and with no resolve to learn; they trusted that the Holy Ghost would enable them to "speak with tongues" instantly in any tongue that they might need. What happened to them I have not heard and dare not ask, but can well imagine. The incident typifies our confusion, even within the Church. The word Ghost suggests an apparition, because we forget that when the King James Version was written the word meant soul or personal entity, as in the saying about the death of Jesus: "He gave up the ghost." [1] The word Spirit also is a bafflement, for the word as used today is as vague as a fog. Add to this bafflement the doctrine of the Trinity, and the result seems "confusion worse confounded." [2]

I

Whence this doctrine? It arose at Pentecost.[3] Christian faith did not coin that name, for Pentecost had long been the name of the Temple celebration of the harvest. The priests lifted high two loaves of wheat in token of thanksgiving. But Pentecost is now the birthday of the Christian Church. That fact should be noted: a festival even deeper in meaning and emotion than our American Thanksgiving, bastioned in the worthy tradition and worship of centuries, is suddenly overwhelmed and transformed. Only an event of power could work such a change. What event? The gift of the Holy Spirit.

The secular world bridles at that account. Many a cult, in orgy of emotion, has "spoken with tongues," even to foaming at the mouth. Glossolalia, the inarticulate mumblings and outcries of primitive religious fervor, is not a new portent. Did not Paul himself warn the church against it? "I would rather speak five words with my mind, in order to instruct others, than ten thousand words in a tongue." [4] As for the "wind" and "fire" at Pentecost, the account of the foundation-laying for the new temple in Jerusalem during the reign of the Emperor Julian tells of whirlwind and earthquake, of balls of fire and star-shaped crosses appearing on the clothes of workmen.[5] Writers in those days were not bound to literal science.

Then what *did* happen at the Christian Pentecost? The Book of Acts reports a sound "as of" a mighty rushing wind, and a wave "as of" fire which divided so that a flame rested on each head.[6] That "as of" admits an imagery. But the imagery was used, not to indulge a fancy, but because the event was so tremendous that it defied prose. Who can describe any rapture, least of all the presence of God? No man in that upper room needed any interpreter for his neighbor's fervor, for all were caught up into one heaven of grace. Nathaniel Hawthorne is surely right when he pleads that the Pentecostal gift was "not the power of speech in foreign and unknown languages, but that of addressing the whole human brotherhood in the heart's native language." [7] That is a mightier miracle.

Let us grant the symbolism of the description; we need not shrink when the author himself confesses it. But let us also realize that such symbolism could have been used only of a revolution in the soul.

> Where I heard noise and you saw flame,
> Some one man knew God called his name.[8]

The "rushing mighty wind" drove away the chaff of life, and the fire consumed the husk. God's speech rested on the lips of mortal men. Then, in the might of the Spirit, they overcame both the seduction of pagan cults and the pride of Roman Empire.

Does someone argue that the Holy Spirit was no new gift? The plea is true: the word Spirit recurs in the Old Testament. "The Spirit of the Lord *clothed Himself* with" Gideon;[9] that is almost the exact Hebrew phrase. The same Spirit brooded over chaos to bring forth the cosmos, or blew on life to wither it. Samson's muscle, David s music, and the artistry of the men who wove the Temple curtains are all ascribed to the Spirit. But Pentecost in the New Testament is still new, for the Spirit of God is there identified with the crucified and risen Jesus. That is the prime meaning. One hundred of His followers were made sure that He is one with God, and present in the hearts of His followers in the love of the Cross and the power of the Resurrection. Pentecost is the gift of *His* Holy Spirit. The New Testament can almost be called the Book of the Holy Spirit. The early church deemed the gift essential: "Did you receive the Holy Spirit when you believed?" [10] It was, and is, not enough to believe in Jesus Christ; for without the Holy Spirit even that belief may become null and void. So we proceed to ask why the gift is essential, since Christ is risen from the dead. What is the meaning and work of the Holy Spirit?

II

The Holy Spirit is *the Interpreter of Jesus*. The record of Jesus' sayings can be read in an hour. They are not in autograph. We now know that they have been edited, as anyone can prove for himself by consulting a harmony of the Gospels, to meet the needs of the early church. Students of the Gospels are thus obliged to delve through strata of interpretation in hope of finding the original word. There is besides an outright loss, for the record gives us only a fraction of all that Jesus said and wrought. What of His word and life before He left Nazareth? What of His comment to Simon of Cyrene as Simon carried His cross? There is an even sadder loss: truth He could not say at all because men's ears are dull: "I have yet many things to say unto you, but ye cannot bear them now." [11]

So the questions multiply: What of the words that Jesus would speak to us were He walking in our world? The high-school principal must exclaim: "If only I knew His mind on education!" The businessman, caught in the inevitable compromises of trade, living in an era when economic systems rise and fall, longs to know what counsel Jesus would give him. Recently a keen-minded journalist said sadly, almost bitterly, "Jesus did not live in a machine age." The statesman, thwarted by iron curtains, burdened by the legacy of two world wars, wonders what guidance Jesus would give in modern statecraft. Where is the answer? It is found in the appendix to that sad remark of Jesus concerning truth He could not tell because men could not hear! This answer: "Howbeit when he, the Spirit of truth, is come, he will guide you into all truth: . . . he shall take of mine, and shall shew it unto you." [12]

The gift of the Spirit is not a promise of absolute guidance. If it were, human freedom would vanish. There are no infallibilities in our mortal world. Prayer does not confer inerrant wisdom. But when men pray, as once a hundred men prayed at Pentecost, they *do* deeply understand the mind of Christ, and light *is* shed upon their path. Thus the early church, tethered in comparative safety to the Jewish synagogue, was moved by the Spirit to preach to the Gentile world. The policy seemed disaster, but "wisdom is justified of her children." [18] Praying men in Germany knew the folly of Hitler, just as praying men in America knew that the Exclusion Act[14] was against the nature of things. The modern church is slow to pray for the guidance of His Spirit and perhaps slower to follow, but even tepid prayer and obedience have brought social passion, ecumenical longing, and a return to the centralities of the faith. The Holy Spirit is the Interpreter of Jesus.

III

The Holy Spirit is *the Apostle of Christ*. If the loss of Christ's teaching seems disastrous, what of the loss of Christ Himself? A hymn sung by the English church tells of a world forlorn without Him:

> But, O dear Lord, we cry,
> That we Thy face could see!
> Thy blessed face one moment's space;
> Then might we follow Thee! [15]

Who has not longed to speak with Jesus, not alone to receive some sure word, but to gather strength from His presence? But He said bluntly, according to the Fourth Gospel, that it was better He should disappear from sight: "It is expedient for you that I go away." [16] The Greek word means not merely expedient, but profitable. Where is the profit? Our eyes can see only loss.

If Jesus were living in our world in the flesh, and if we knew Him for Saviour (as we might not), not many people could be His close friends. The rich could travel, and might try to adopt Him, until they learned His rigor. Crowds would throng. His followers would run to Him at every turn of decision. We might become as children, living by the rote of His command. We might walk in bondage to eyes and ears. That, surely, is why He said: "I will pray the Father, and he shall give you another Comforter . . . for . . . he shall be in you." [17] It is better to know that Christ lives in me than that Christ lives in the flesh on my street. The gift of the Spirit is that more wonderful grace. It is a miracle that Christ is not forgotten. His death was ignominy; and even His resurrection was no planetary lightning to blind and compel mankind, but a Gentleness that cheered two lonely men on the Emmaus Road.[18] Why *is* He remembered? Every man denies Him many times in a day; and as for our social greeds, they blatantly mock Him. Then why does He not pass into oblivion? Why is His cross on the jewelry tray at Tiffany's—and Woolworth's? Why are we brought to stillness when we see His picture? Because a promise has been fulfilled: the Holy Spirit is given. "He shall glorify me." [19] "He will convince the world of sin and of righteousness and of judgment." [20] That English hymn has the proper climax:

> Within our heart of hearts
> In nearest nearness be:
> Set up Thy throne within Thine own:
> Go, Lord, we follow Thee.[21]

This is a new kind of sculpture: Christ fashions us, not from without by word and gesture, but from within by indwelling Presence.

IV

Thus the Holy Spirit is *the Inspirer of mankind* in wisdom, courage, and love. Sometimes the New Testament uses the name Comforter—con-fort, with strength. The Greek noun translated "Comforter" is *Paraclētos,* a word hard to translate, meaning perhaps (as we have already suggested) Helper or Apostle. The King James Version once translates the same Greek *Paraclētos* by "advocate." [22] In the Roman courts an *advocatus* was one who stood by an accused man to defend and strengthen him. Another New Testament name for the Holy Spirit is *Pneuma,* meaning breath, almost as that word is used in the hymn: "Breathe on me, Breath of God." [23] Whatever the name, there is promise of wisdom, courage, and love beyond man's native endowment; and the promise has been fulfilled.

As for wisdom, surely that quickening has come in preaching and architecture, in music and art. The earliest followers of Jesus understood Him better after His death than in the days of His flesh. Well might Handel say of his "Hallelujah Chorus" that it seemed to him as if heaven had been opened.[24] It had, by the gift of Christ's Spirit. Again and again in the onsets of life the right word has sprung to Christian lips: "It shall be given you in that same hour what ye shall speak." [25] This is no pledge that missionaries going to China or India shall instantly speak the language. The promise was given to men who were committed to Christ by study, prayer, and venture. It means that if we discipline ourselves in Christ, we shall not be unbefriended in the crisis. If we have no chance to prepare the word for Christ, it will be given. There is a nice instance in the story of Francis of Assisi. He boldly visited Malik-al-Kamil, the enemy of the Church, to plead for peace. But the emperor had prepared a cruel jest for God's "poor little man": the carpet in the royal tent was woven with the pattern of the Cross, in a day when men believed that anyone treading on the Cross would be cursed! So Francis unwittingly trampled on the sign of his dearest faith. But when the sultan laughed, and Francis saw the ugly joke, his answer was instant: "There were three crosses on Calvary!" [26] Wisdom, through slow discipline and through instant word, is the gift of the Spirit.

As for valor, Pentecost proved it within an hour; for Peter, who a few days earlier had cravenly denied his Lord, now fearlessly confronted the same kind of mob that had cried, "Crucify!" We read the record of Christian martyrdom and wonder at a bravery that seems to go beyond flesh and blood. There is no "seems"; it did go beyond mortal sinew. The victims of Nero died in no mere stoicism, and in no mere hardihood of the flesh, but in radiance of soul. Persecuted Christians in Madagascar, flung from a high cliff to their death in the sea, were heard singing hymns as they fell. Many an unbeliever has died stolidly, or with iron nerve, or unconcernedly in the rush of anger and excitement; but the death of the martyrs is of another order. It is inspiration: "You shall receive power when the Holy Spirit has come upon you." [27]

As for love, that change was more striking even than the transformation of dullness into vision, or of cowardice into valor. There was *esprit de corps* in the early church —or, rather, *Esprit de corps*. They were rich and poor, learned and ignorant, bond and free, young and old, sinners and saints. These divergencies still mark the Church. No other group would dare risk them. But the Church can risk them, for the Church is indwelt by one Spirit. The early church had all things in common. The communism was quite voluntary and in Christ, and therefore puts to shame the dreary modern version. The present church is still indwelt by a common Love. The church I serve is a cross section not only of social groups, but even of national and racial groups. By any human test it should suffer from locomotor ataxia—its limbs should be out of control. But it is remarkably one in the Spirit, and would be even more united, as would any church, were it more consecrate in prayer and witness. The Christian Church is sometimes stuffy and timid to a fault. Yet for Love's sake it has girded the earth with schools and hospitals and kindling worship. What other group can claim any comparable harvest? Thus the followers of Christ have often heard the gospel proclaimed "every man in his own tongue," in the universal language of the Spirit of Christ. At Babel,[28] the city of man's pride, "confusion of tongues" fell on our world; at Pentecost, city of the Spirit, the confusion was redeemed in a love so instantly wise that every man knew his neighbor's heart. Leonard Hodgson is surely right: the answer to cults that talk vaguely of "the spirit of love" is an outright avowal of the doctrine of the Holy Spirit.[29]

V

Then what of belief in the Trinity? Alien minds call it a "mathematical puzzle." But few theologians have been intent on formulas. God is Mystery, even though He is incarnate in Jesus Christ. The doctrines of the Church compass the Mystery of God even less than maps of early explorers of America compassed that unexplored continent. The explorers knew only the shore they touched. Even there the knowledge was dim. Yet they had touched a real continent. So we touch Reality, and we must make maps, if only in compassion for those who follow us. Men have sensed God in His creation, not least in His creation of their own life; men have sensed God in Jesus Christ; men have sensed God in the moving of His Spirit. This "sensing" is undeniable experience, and the doctrine of the Trinity is an attempt, clumsy but inevitable and not untrue, to transcribe that experience in a creed. A creed, though all creeds are but explorers' maps, reflects experience; and therefore helps to renew the experience for the redemption of man's life.

This fact also is pertinent: only in mathematics can a single unity be found, and mathematics is an abstraction. In life, as contrasted with abstraction, unity is always multiple unity. A finger is not unity, for it belongs to a hand; a hand is not unity, for it belongs to an arm;

an arm is not unity, for it belongs to a body; a man is not unity, for he could not live except by a family. The higher we rise in the scale of life, from a stone to a tree to a man, the more definitely we see that unity is multiple unity. The critics should speak of the "mathematical puzzle" called man, for the true human unit is the family. Furthermore this multiplicity in unity is a mark of all creative mind. The *Unfinished Symphony* first existed in the mind of Schubert and there lived its own life; then it became incarnate in a score written on paper and in sounds produced by instruments; then it became a spirit, so that a music lover in Australia can write to a music lover in Norway and ask—without any need to play the music for confirmation—how and why the third movement was never written.

Thus the doctrine of the Trinity, though it adumbrates a Mystery, is not incongruous with the whole mystery of man's life. It answers human need. We worship God in His creation as our Father; we worship God in His Incarnation in Christ, and claim His pardon; we worship God in the Holy Spirit, rejoicing that, instead of our being bereaved by the exaltation of Christ, we are indwelt by His presence. The mystics have sometimes dared to speak of "The Family of the Godhead." They know, and are blessed, while others who captiously speak of the "hairsplitting of theologians" still move in shallowness. Why not launch out into the mighty deep of faith? There is life in the adoring "Holy, Holy, Holy" of the doctrine of the Trinity.

VI

Everyone now knows that the prime need of our world is a new spirit, but few are yet aware that the word must be spelled with a capital *S*. Man's spirit alone, even at best, cannot save us. Our "defenses" are still only a competition in armaments, for "defense" itself implies a cleavage in the human family; and the competition has now reached the stage where all human life is under threat. Our learning has not taught us how to live together, because it has not taught us how to live with God; and all learning is ambushed by the dark irrationality that erupts from the depths of life, so scientific rationalism in Germany had no bulwark against Hitler's cult of "blood and soil." Our power to organize is only an engine without a spark and without any intelligent driver, until light and power come from Beyond.

What we need is enthusiasm in the literal meaning of the word—"in God." Pentecost turned blindness into sight, fear into a valor that was careless of death, and selfishness into love; for Pentecost was the gift of the Spirit of Christ. The gift is never a sinecure: Pentecost brought bodily risk to the hundred gathered to pray. But it brought also the ultimate security of God's presence. Our skills and knowledge need a new main contact:

> Come, Holy Ghost, our souls inspire;
> And lighten with celestial fire.[30]

Then what to do? No man can command God; He is not at our casual beck and call. Who can command the wind?

But a man may dispose himself to receive the wind, as a sailor may be ready with sail unfurled. The same conditions that governed Pentecost govern our world; the same response would bring the same blessing. One hundred men in our time could lead the same radiant revolution in the same Spirit. Therefore look again at Pentecost.

VII

They were thinking about Jesus. At His behest they waited "for the promise" [31] of His coming. As they tarried, they pondered His life and death. Does someone say that *we* cannot imagine Him, because we have not seen Him in the flesh? It would be truer to say that everyone *does* imagine Him, and that every man's imagining is different from his neighbor's, and that every imagining may still be true. If you saw a new picture of Jesus, you would be disappointed in it, however glowing its portrayal, because you would *know* that it fell far short of His glory. His Spirit enables every man to think of Him. Only so could any thought of Him survive in our dull and devilish world. But as long as our minds are full of schemes and machines, money and politics, bricks and publicities, to the forgetting of Christ, we shall cry in vain for a new Pentecost. They were thinking about Jesus at Pentecost.

They were praying, not for the fulfillment of their desires, but that Christ would newly come. We have ceased to believe in prayer, whatever lip service we may still offer. Our phrases betray us. "We can still pray" means that no sensible man would use so blunt a weapon until all sharper swords are broken. "We can at least pray" means just what it says—that in our eyes prayer is among the least of all our acts. But Christ spoke of prayer as if life depended on it, because life *does* depend on it. Prayer is not a last resort, as with the condemned man who, when he heard word of his reprieve, flung his prayer book to the other end of his cell. Prayer is opening a door to the power of God. Waiting in prayer is like the gathering of a great river behind a dam: soon fertility shall come to the fields, soon power shall turn a thousand wheels, soon light shall bless hamlet and city. They were praying at Pentecost. Perhaps other means are denied our time that we may relearn the royal way of prayer.

They were ready to follow the leading of the Spirit. Why should guidance ever be given if we are unready to obey? "He will *guide* you into all truth" [32] —there is no coercion. The men of Pentecost ventured—in new paths. A five-year contract between a major industrial corporation and a major union is in the guidance of the Spirit, granted the spark of Pentecostal fire, for it substitutes a resolve to understand for the endless circle of conflict. The United Nations, provided the flame falls from Heaven, is the Spirit's alternative to the suicide of competitive arms. The Spirit at Pentecost sent men on unwonted paths, at cost, and they obeyed; and their obedience was a new opening for a yet greater gift of the Spirit. Should we not say to many a politician, even to some leaders in the Church: "You have nothing but an old word, even though the world is manifestly in change, even though the old word has baptized our world in blood"? Pentecost gives courage, but only for a new and hazardous path.

VIII

The Joel prophecy,[33] which the early church linked with Pentecost, promised that the gift of the Spirit should fall upon "all flesh." It would be no sacerdotal monopoly, but a grace bestowed on young and old, masters and servants, parents and children. There were a hundred people in that upper room. Presumably not more than eleven had intimately walked with Christ. But the other eighty-nine received a like grace. A flame rested on each head. God is eager that the "lost sayings" of Jesus shall be spoken through us, and that words He could not speak in the flesh because of the hardness of men's hearts shall now find utterance through us. All that is asked is that we think on Christ, pray for His coming, and follow where His Spirit leads. When we obey, the tumult of our time will become daybreak instead of doom. A friend camping with Hilaire Belloc in the Pyrenees, terrified when an early morning gale overturned their tent, cried: "Is this the end of the world?" Belloc, who knew that country well, reassured him: "This is how dawn comes in the Pyrenees!" [34] Granted a new Pentecost we might say of the turmoil of our time: "This is how dawn comes —with the 'sound as of a rushing mighty wind' and a wave 'as of fire.' "

CHAPTER V

Faith in the Church

"I speak concerning Christ and the church."
Ephesians 5:32

MOST PEOPLE do not believe in the Church; their scorn or indifference speaks for itself. Perhaps most church members do not really believe in the Church. If they were asked what can solve mankind's present impasse, the word church might not even occur to them, let alone come eagerly to their lips. We have noted in Chapter I the comment of the magazine reporter to his editor: "People want to believe something. But what? They look at the church, then look away again—it is not there." The church on the next corner hardly fits the description given in the New Testament; the "church of the firstborn, which are written in heaven." [1]

Why should the Church become an article of belief? Faith in God, in Christ, perhaps in the Holy Spirit, we can understand; but faith in the Church seems like leaning on a rickety fence above a precipice. "The church down the road?" we ask with raised eyebrows. "Where Bill Whoosiz passes the collection plate?" Usually the church down the road is dubious in architecture; and some of its hymns do not qualify either as poetry or music, let alone as awe-filled worship. These are the slighter disfigurements. The Church is worldly, stained by the common customs of mankind, intent on numbers and prestige; so that Robert G. Ingersoll's gibe has its truth: "The church has always been willing to swap off treasures in heaven for cash down." [2] The Church is divided, not only to the bafflement of John Doe, who cannot understand either the varieties or the reasons given for them, but to the mocking of Christ's prayer "that they all may be one." [3] The Church is blind: it has stayed the march of truth, even with bloody persecutions. The Church is craven: it rarely stands for the unpopular right; it knows little of the valorous abandon of the Cross.

I

Of course these charges are too sweeping to be just. There is always a Church within the Church, like the fructifying core within a grain of wheat. Some in the Church are not worldly: they count the world well lost for Christ. Some are not divisive: they pray that there may be "one fold, and one Shepherd." [4] Some are not blind: they welcome truth and are its first prophets. Some are not craven: the Church has been rich in martyrs. Always there is a spring of life within the Church.

If the noble music, architecture, and art of the Church were suddenly removed, the history of the last nineteen hundred years would resemble a picture with a fist driven through it—its meaning and worth would largely be lost. Some missionaries have been angular and bigoted; and some have not, for soldiers in World War II found in faraway corners men and women of culture and friendliness on lonely duty in a nobler war—the crusade for Christ. The missionary endeavor as a whole is now disclosed as an astonishing campaign; for the Church, with little money and less repute, has set the gentleness of hospital, the light of schools, and the saving grace of Christ's worship across our world, like a multitude of stars in a dark sky. Again, why this spring of life?

As for the local church, though it seems as incongruous in any roster of Christian convictions as a hobo at a symphony concert, the same fount of renewal redeems its drabness. Store windows richly decked appeal to our acquisitiveness, yet business must advertise to sell its wares. Theaters and movies, with varied arts for ally, appeal to our senses; but they are often hard pressed to win a crowd, as witness "give-away programs." But the church, perhaps with dull sermons, casual worship, and leadership far from saintly, lives on through every crisis, while industries and empires topple to the fall. Again, what *is* this secret of life?

The secret shows in a saving grace of self-criticism. Political parties rarely admit failure, though they have wide opportunity; they "point with pride," even though the pointing finger shows nothing but emptiness. Manufacturers' associations do not confess guilt, though they must carry a share of blame for eras of unemployment and the pittance wages of slum-darkened cities. Labor unions do not beat upon their breasts, though they are slow to find a better goal than wages and hours, and are blind to the fact that the urgent issue is the nature of the work. But the Church's guilt is ever before it; and the Church is excoriated most unsparingly, not by its atheistic critics, but in its own house. This fact is part of a wider fact: in an age of standardized opinion the Church, with whatever failure, is an island of genuine freedom. Again, why this persistent life? The Church, by any human test, should long ago have disappeared. Paganisms and persecutions without, and worse treacheries within, should have wiped it from the map. But it is like the church at Walton-on-the-Naze in England. The sea encroached and drowned it, and people soon forgot; but one day an unusually low tide disclosed it, apparently cleansed by streaming waters of baptism.[5] The Church is more than a man in the pulpit or men in the pew. What *is* its hidden spring?

II

The Church is the *home of the worship of God* the Father. Thus it is right that the avowal of faith in God should be linked with the avowal of faith in the Church. As the Church thus gives itself to God in worship, the life of God flows back into the Church. So the Church survives in strength always renewed. Worship requires a building, even though the church is not mere windows and stone. "Requires" is the word, for we cannot long worship God in the out-of-doors, despite our pretense. There are too many distractions in the countryside: the honk of automobiles, the roar of airplanes, not to mention the unsightliness of billboards. Besides, nature cannot kindle truest worship, despite sunrise services; for nature has reptiles among its flowers and earthquakes below its harvest fields. Musicians are not so foolish as to learn music from nature, as some would-be religionists propose to learn God. Musicians build walls to make a silence, and there gather the music scores of the masters plus the skill of worthy teachers. Musicians thus trained may then have ears for the music of nature. So the Church builds walls to shut out the distractions of earth. There it gathers man's best witness to God—the Bible, hymns and prayers that have been born of faith, such teaching as men can give, and the sign of the Cross for surety of the Presence. When people thus worship, they are afterward able to trace God in nature. The worship of God requires a building, reverent yet lowly, rigorous yet beautiful, even more than human love requires a home.

The Church as surely requires membership. The canard "I can worship better alone" should be nailed down as nonsense. It would not be more foolish to say "A nose can be a better nose without a face," or "A child can be a better child without a family." For a man can do nothing alone, much less do it better. If a man were alone, he would die. Robinson Crusoe would have been helpless on his island had he not first learned communal arts, and Man Friday was no misfortune, and after a few years Robinson was glad to return to London. There is place for private prayer, for every man is a single soul: "When thou prayest, enter into thy closet, and when thou hast shut thy door, pray to thy Father which is in secret." [6] But we are false to Jesus and to life if we twist that counsel into a denial of corporate worship; for Jesus also said "Where two or three are gathered together"— the phrase means precisely a corporate worship—"there am I in the midst." [7] Corporate worship would die without private prayer, as a tree would die if every leaf were always torn from it; but private prayer would die without corporate worship, as a leaf would die if bereft of its tree. Private and corporate prayer are in complement. Corporate worship is not arithmetic of addition; it is repeated mutual multiplication, so that "one loving heart sets another on fire" [8] in the gift of a Divine flame.

Let no man discount worship. It is not ecclesiastical trimming; it is vital breath. To explain it as the mercenary invention of far-off priests (surely one of the shallowest of our modern shoals of thought!) is rather worse than explaining music as an unfortunate noise foisted on mankind by the greed of the first salesmen of musical instruments. Nobody contrived the word God: we found it on our lips because God hid it in our hearts. We could make a pun, halfway between a sob and a gladness, about a spire: it is there because we a-spire. As successful men return unsatisfied to the village of their boyhood, yearning for an unspoiled heart, so men return to the primal purity of God. It is a poor simile, for a man *must* return to God or court inward death. So ineradicable is the urge to worship, so indispensable the Church, that if we do not worship God, we begin to worship ourselves or our neighbors. Modern skepticism has not ceased to worship—it sets up as idol a physics laboratory or a skyscraper, or it makes some Lenin its god. Thus only a true worship can redeem us from the civil war of our egotisms.

Now we can understand a fructifying persistence in the Church. Other groups are only cisterns soon broken; the Church is a flowing spring, for in its acknowledgment of God it receives a pristine life. The cisterns have their place, but they are still useless without the flowing spring. Human power has some gift: it can unclog the spring and channel it, but not create or contrive it, for it is God's gift. Assuredly we cannot live without Him. To worship the reservoir or the plumbing would be insane, but not more insane than our worship of man's skill and knowledge to the forgetting of their primal Source. Does someone argue that many people get along quite well without worship? Berlin and Hiroshima, not to mention the fear and frenzy of "enlightened lands," are poor evidence. People do not live without worship: they die. They sink below themselves when they cease to worship One above themselves.

III

The Church is *the home of the grace of Christ.* Thus the Church is rightly linked with Christ in our deepest faith. A plea could be made that Christ is not the monopoly of the Church. True, but the Church is the monopoly of Christ—His "body," the new incarnation of His Spirit. Many groups try to use Christ. Editorials include His name to prove a case, quite unaware of the mild blasphemy. Politicians quote Him in the perorations of speeches, as if Christ could be lackey to a political campaign. Military men try to use Him, to gird military morale. But the Church *worships* Him. The Church is used *by* Him, who nevertheless has such love that He could not "use" anyone. The Church *exists for* Christ and without Him has no ground or growth.

So the Church mediates the *judgment* of Christ. A Los Angeles man spent two years carving a tiny replica of a church in Ulm, Germany.[9] He made a toy church, and it was his to own. Even church members try to treat the real Church, Christ's Church, as a pastime. But His Church carries judgment, for it holds Him before the eyes of our disfigured world. The word for church in classical Greek means at its root those who are *called out from* the world. We need not be surprised that the Church is reproached. As often as His name is spoken, especially in prayer, our common life is condemned— the ugliness of politics and trade, not noticeable in the shadows of the world's accepted standards, are laid bare in His light. Then the world turns angrily on the Church with "Do *you* follow Him?" The Church can answer only, "No; so you and I together must seek His pardon, for darkness falls if we deny His light." What would happen if there were no sign of judgment? A far worse chaos than if there were no alternate night and day, no sky to correct our clocks. The world hardly needs to condemn the Church, for every church is condemned by the Christ it proclaims. Yet that fact is more reason, not less, for the proclamation of the gospel. The Church must open the door to the light, even though its own shabbiness is thus exposed, for mankind cannot live without light. How blind the man in the pew who shrinks from sharp judgment in the pulpit! He should rather thank God, lest "old night" come upon the world!

By the same token the Church mediates the *mercy* of Christ. For His judgment is mercy, as light is both judgment and mercy to men who have lived in gloom. Had the Church no word but judgment, it would be prophet of despair; but light, though pain at first, is healing and joy. The next chapter asks how history is cleansed. The remedy cannot come by man. Who among us can renew a war-bombed city as if the bombs had not fallen? We cannot return to mend the broken past, for life moves in one direction; we can neither stay nor reverse its course. If we could return, we could not mend the brokenness but might repeat it; for the brokenness is in the sinew of our will. God alone can mend history, for He alone holds past, present, and future in one creative span. Only God entering history can mend history. There are no parables, except in distant hint for such mercy. What would be the parable? A doctor, assured in livelihood and honored in practice, deliberately choosing to go to a doctorless and plague-infested town? The hint would still be pale and remote—for soul sickness cannot be healed by man, and man cannot pay the price called Calvary, and no doctor can assure cure as God in Christ assures pardon to all who will receive it. The Church can only mediate the mercy of Christ, but that mediation is yet mankind's best gift—the offering of a channel for God's grace.

The Church is the proper channel for that mercy, for Christ finds his best opening in the worship that esteems Him all in all. There His Spirit has free course. So the world learns of Christ through the Church. We could not have heard of Him otherwise, except perhaps in rumor or in the cold record of distant history. The novel *Magnificent Obsession*,[10] almost suggests that the hero, Dr. Hudson, came on his secret by chance, or that it fell on him "as the gentle rain from heaven":[11] "Let not thy left hand know what thy right hand doeth." [12] The Church does not cut much figure in the story. But Dr. Hudson actually learned his secret from the author, who is a Christian minister; and *he* doubtless learned it through some church school or church. We sometimes hear it said that a man is "a Christian, though he never darkens the door of a church." The verdict is probably untrue, for no man can be radiantly Christian without the experience of corporate worship. But, even if the verdict were true, the man could not have been a Christian unless *someone* had darkened the door of a church. The man at best is a parasitic Christian. The Church is the indispensable comradeship: it is the home of the grace of "our Lord Jesus Christ."

IV.

The Church is the *home of the communion of the Holy Spirit,* and therefore of "the communion of saints." For Christian worship is not offered to a remote God or to a Christ who once lived on earth, but in and through the eternal Spirit. At birth most babes come into a home; they find welcome in a spirit of love. At a man's new birth in Christ he finds welcome in a better home. In this church home Christians are married, for our earthly homes do not stand except in the eternal grace; they cannot live on themselves, any more than a man could feed on his own flesh. In this home Christians are laid to rest when "travelling days are done," [13] for only their bodies are committed to the ground; their souls are given in the Holy Spirit to the care of God. How has the Church survived? The local church through which I serve, in the middle of Manhattan Island, has outstayed in its history six wars and six financial panics. What business or government can make such a claim? The Church has more than human power—the indwelling life of the Spirit of God.

We need not shy away from the phrase "the communion of saints." For "saints" does not mean haloed people who are comfortable only in stained-glass windows. Still less does it imply self-righteous people critical of their ungodly neighbors. Perhaps most of the saints in the calendar would not be easy companions on a fishing trip. But the "saints" mentioned in the New Testament were not in the calendar—they were in the Church: "All the saints salute you, chiefly they that are of Caesar's household." [14] A free but not untrue translation would read: "All the good folk in Christ send greetings, especially the slaves in the imperial palace." "Saints" in New Testament parlance are homespun folk who are committed to Christ because they know His love has redeemed them. People sometimes refuse to join the church because they are "not good enough." If they really mean "because I am not yet ready to commit myself in life-loyalty to Jesus," they do well to delay; but if they mean "because I have not yet reached a sufficient measure of saintliness by my own striving," they make no sense, for no man can reach saintliness on his own account. People should join a church, not because they are good enough, but because they know they are not good enough: they join a church as confessed sinners who have accepted by faith God's pardon offered in Jesus Christ. Is it strange that the Church is unworthy? It exists for unworthy folk. Day by day it receives sinners into a love made known in Jesus. No other fellowship would risk such a promiscuous inflow. The Church invites and seeks it because the Church is the home of the cleansing of the Holy Spirit. In that sense it is "the communion of saints."

The communion erases all the dividing lines of earth. It flows around and holds all lands, as ocean flows around continents and islands. Granted that the Church has been tinctured by national and racial prejudice, the fact remains that from the first the Church has been a worldwide fellowship. Is there any other social solvent? What other group welcomes and incorporates all ages, all levels of better and worse, all grades of learning and ignorance, all lands and races? No other group *could* welcome them, for only the Church believes outrightly that the common denominator of human life is nothing human at all, but the moving and indwelling Spirit of God. The Cyclorama at Atlanta,[15] a portrayal in oil of one episode of our American Civil War, shows a soldier in Northern uniform tending a dying soldier in Confederate uniform. Their faces are strikingly alike—they were brothers. But the Church knows that men are brothers though their faces and color of skin are not alike, for the Church exalts a deeper alikeness—their alikeness in God's love, the only bond that can make "one world." In this sense also the Church is "the communion of saints."

And in a deeper sense: it is the communion of saints in earth and heaven. Every social group fractures, and thus fails its members. A home is broken both by unworthiness and death. Systems "have their day and cease to be." [16] Cities disfigure their citizens by mean streets, earthy strivings, and the pressures of mass anonymity. Every group loyalty on our earth leaves its members bereft at last. But the Church is not merely on our earth: it lives in the worship of God, the grace of Christ, and the communion of the Holy Spirit. Its loyalty binds it to the sky as well as to the earth. Its bonds are with eternity as well as with time. So its members are not left bankrupt. When Savonarola was about to be martyred for heresy, the accusing bishop of Vasona bungled the customary formula, "I deprive you of the church militant"; for he added, "and the church triumphant." The martyr rightly replied: "Of the church militant, yes; but of the church which is triumphant, no; that does not belong to you." [17]

In point of fact, not even the church militant belonged to the bishop, but only to God. Moreover the church militant and the church triumphant are indissolubly one Church. Hymns about heaven can become saccharine, but properly they are the expression of a rich and requisite faith:

> Yet she on earth hath union
> With Father, Spirit, Son,
> And mystic sweet communion
> With those whose rest is won.[18]

The Church is the abiding and inviolable comradeship, for the Church is the home of the Holy Spirit, "the communion of saints."

V

Let us admit that the Church has failed. That failure is in one sense not surprising: the Church exists for failures and is composed of failures. Let us admit that the Church has failed in a more tragic sense: it has subtly turned to self-trust instead of trusting only to the grace of God made known in Jesus Christ. Even so the reporter who said, "They look at the church, then look away again," told of an unwisdom. No one need "look away again," for only the Church within the Church confesses failure, and only the Church has the secret spring of renewal.

Has the Church really failed? Its severest critics use a Christian criterion to condemn the Church. That is a startling fact: the real charge against the Church is that it has betrayed its Lord. Then has the Church completely failed? It has given the standard of judgment to its critics, and made that standard the currency of the world. New life will break forth from the Church. Its hope is the root of every other hope. But where does the critic's charge leave the critic? He blames the Church for stumbling on a high hard road, while he himself stays in the valley. Thus a friend, when someone refuses to join the church because "there are too many hypocrites," is fond of replying: "Don't let that deter you; there is always room for one more."

Only two honorable roads are open to a man who believes with even half-faith in Jesus. One is to join the church and from within speak His judgment to purify its life: "Faithful are the wounds of a friend."[19] The other is to build a better church. As for that latter course, the attempts have been legion, shabby, and caught in swift death, because every such pioneer must begin with the same human nature (people like you and me), his first move being a critical revolt, not unlike the revolt of a tree against its roots. The roots are not completely dry: "There is a river, the streams whereof shall make glad the

city of God." [20] The Church is the home of the worship of
God, the only safeguard against a grotesque self-worship,
and the only fulfillment of life. The Church is the home
of the grace of Christ, without whom we have no master-
light and no salvation from demonism. The Church is
the home of the communion of the Holy Spirit: there is no
other bond in whom heaven and earth can become home;
for only so can there be a fellowship of "saints"—the folk
of every land and generation who, aware that they are
loved of Christ, love Him in return, and thus are able
to love mankind—looking to eternal life.

CHAPTER VI

Faith in Forgiveness

"Be it known unto you therefore, men and bret-
ren, that through this man is preached unto you the
forgiveness of sins."   Acts 13:38

TWO COLLEGE GIRLS were overheard discussing a
lecture on the Atonement. As they walked from the audi-
torium, one said, "He kept talking about sin, but what
did he mean?" The other replied, "Oh, that has something to do with Adam and Eve." I can vouch for the incident, for I was the clumsy lecturer, and a friend was the
reporter. The word sin has lost meaning. Perhaps the
Church, including the lecturer, is partly to blame; for its
doctrinal words call for reinterpretation in the thought
forms of each new generation, and the Church neglects
that task. Perhaps our generation is partly to blame for
the girls' bafflement: it has studied the cosmos rather than
the soul, and has tried to whittle responsibility into mere
"frustration."

Yet the girls were baffled only by the word; they understood the fact. If the Easter finery of one had been filched,
she would not have said, "This is a scientific fact to be
studied"; and if the other's fiancé had been alienated by a

mendacious rival, she would not easily or sensibly have said, "My rival is psychologically frustrated, and a lie is not really a lie." Crime is a breach of the public law, and sin might be defined as a breach of God's law. Both definitions are vulnerable. For prophets sometimes break the public law from above it, as Jesus broke the religious law of his day, to bring a worthier law; and, as for God's law, that is too cold a term, for sin is the grieving of His Spirit. Yet both definitions have pith.

We should distinguish carefully between God's law and man's reading of it, for the two are frequently confused. We may question the reading, but may not deny the law. Psychology, for instance, can help shrewdly in correcting man's reading, but should hold no brief for the denial. Eliminating error from a compass is wisdom; flouting the magnetic north is folly. A man might worthily argue; "Jean Valjean's original theft of bread for a hungry home, or even his subsequent bitter theft of the bishop's silver,[1] was more his misfortune than his guilt"; but that verdict could not justly go further to say: "There are no standards of right and wrong." For the word "misfortune" there implies condemnation of the society that makes hungry homes, sends Jean Valjean to the galleys, and by its lovelessness provokes him to bitterness on his release. To declare that "right and wrong are only relative" only darkens wisdom with words. To what or whom are they relative? If they are relative to what is relative, in endless emptiness of relativity, there are no standards; and that lack would rob life of any meaning. Granted that our reading of God's law is often distorted, and that pity should sometimes replace our blame, the law remains. A friend owns a fragment of Grecian marble that was probably carved by Phidias. He could destroy it without committing a crime, for he owns it. But he could not destroy it without committing sin, for in that act he would not only hurt mankind, but violate Beauty—the ultimate standard that men call God. We all disfigure life, a more precious wealth than a Phidias statue. We are sinners.

I

Sin is the reverse sign of worth. No man could deface a Phidias statue if the sense of beauty were not in him. Any doctrine of the "fall" proclaims man's prior height. Our cat would despoil the wren's nest on the next porch if we gave him chance; yet he would not be guilty, because he has no sense of right and wrong. But if a man were to destroy the nest without just reason, he would be wanton and a vandal; for he "knows better," because he knows the Best. Jesus said, "If you were blind, you would have no guilt; but now that you say, 'We see,' your guilt remains." [2] Thus the word sinner, though spoken in condemnation, is an awe-filled word; for it implies that the sinner is potentially the child of God. Those college girls, had they understood the word sin, need not have taken umbrage; for the word sinner always means "You could be a saint."

That is why sin brings remorse. We worry over the shameful past, and to that measure we are noble. All great

literature—*King Lear* [3] and *The Brothers Karamazov* [4]
are only peer instances in an illustrous host—testifies to
man's remorse. To whittle sin into "frustration" discredits
man. The attempt cannot long succeed, for it goes counter to our nature.

> He that wrongs his friend
> Wrongs himself more, and ever bears about
> A silent court of justice in his breast,
> Himself the judge and jury, and himself
> The prisoner at the bar, ever condemn'd.
> And that drags down his life. [5]

Tennyson there was not accurate, for no man can be both
judge and prisoner, unless beyond man's judgment God
stands as Judge of all men. There are extenuations in
every sin, but despite every extenuation the sin remains,
for that is what we extenuate; and the sin brings weary
sorrow. Behind psychological "maladjustment," behind
the defiance and tragic disharmony of our age, behind
the dismaying headlines of our newspapers there is sin—
man's grieving of God's Spirit.

The remorse carries a conviction of helplessness. Man
cannot of himself mend sin's breach. Buddhism does not
explain how a cankered will, especially when by punishment it falls into a lower incarnation, can lift itself back
to a lost height. No man can reverse time to remove a
deceit practiced ten years ago; and if he could, the deceit
is now in him to vitiate his pure resolve. Our attempts at
self-salvation always fail. We keep busy, but find no peace.
We try a long vacation in Florida, but unfortunately we

must take ourselves on the journey. We determine on a high morality, but there is sackcloth beneath the white robe and the morality may become self-righteousness. We try to bargain with God by gifts to charity, as men in ancient days offered their children on an appeasing altar, but we secretly know that God would not be God were He open to such barter. We hope that sin and remorse will die of old age, only to find that one swift second of memory can resurrect the past. No man can cure his own guilt. No man can forgive himself unless he is first forgiven of God. In this issue, as in all else, man's life is linked with his Creator.

The mention of ancient altars brings reminder of a moving chapter in man's story. Only silliness could brand an altar as mere superstition. The sacrifice had to be worthy, such as a firstling of the flock; the smoke carried man's prayers to the mysterious sky; the fire, so Jewish faith believed, was kindled by God. Why an altar? Because man dimly surmised even then that only heaven can cleanse the stains of earth. The cult of the scapegoat carries the same pathos. The animal driven off into the wilderness, bearing the dreadful burden of man's sin, is token of a faith that Mercy out there in the unknown can absorb man's blackness. Every altar, however blood-soaked, is a sign of man's awareness that his sin is an ultimate breach, and that therefore only God can deal with it. Such "superstition" has deeper truth, for all its distortions, than an "intelligence" that trusts only to man's poor wisdom.

FAITH IN FORGIVENESS

Every altar is eloquent of the hope of pardon. Sinful man believes there is some worth in him that ought to be treasured. So he searches the natural world for sign of forgiveness. He notices that the litter of a village carnival is soon covered by meadow grass, and that harvests wave on ground lately torn by the red carnival of war. He searches his own nature for the same sign, and notices that human beings have learned to forgive. It is a rare grace, and never perfect. "Nobuddy ever forgits where he buried a hatchet," said the rural philosopher Abe Martin.[6] Yet an Armenian nurse did tend with care the Turkish soldier who massacred her helpless brother. Yes, her motive was learned of Christ; but, even so, there is impulse in human nature to forgive. A group of Hindu youths, hearing for the first time the injunctions of the Sermon on the Mount—"Love your enemies, bless them that curse you, do good to them that hate you"[7]—exclaimed, "Oh, how beautiful! How divine! This is the truth!" But the signs of pardon in nature and human nature are cloudy and few; not by them can we be sure of pardon.

II

Perhaps we have cleared enough ground now for a building of faith. Every man sins; his sin is the concave of his godliness and therefore brings remorse; he is helpless to mend the past, yet longs for pardon. Now we may ask how forgiveness is found. Here is the first fact: *God must provide it.* There is double reason for this avowal. As for the one item: our sin is locked in the past, though still present in our memory, and only God can change the past. Napoleon, after one of his battles, saw among the dead a colonel with whom he had lately quarreled. Looking down at the crumpled body he exclaimed: "I regret not having been able to speak to him before the battle, in order to tell him that I had long forgotten everything." [8] That regret haunts all of us, but we cannot bring the dead past to life to cleanse away its stains. As for the other item: sin is against God, and for that reason also only God can forgive. Though a man sins against himself, he is a creature; and therefore he sins more deeply against the Creator. Our phrases "antisocial" and "failure in community" are true, but only proximate, for an offense against the comradeship is a sharper wound inflicted on Him in whom all communities are born and held. A lie is not merely a breach in community: it is a lie, a sin against Truth. So for a double reason—man's inability to cleanse history, and the fact that all sin is against God—only God can forgive.

Underscore the second fact: *we must see God forgiving in our world,* or we can neither believe in nor accept pardon. The scapegoat was a liturgy, not uninspired, by which man could see the work of pardon. An altar likewise was in ancient Israel the visible sign of an invisible Grace. But the language we best understand is the language of our own daily life. Pardon is not a mere parchment of reprieve. It is more than an edict from a Throne. It does indeed wipe away the stain; but it must do more, or invite new and worse stains. Pardon is a gift of new life, through the pain and persistence of incarnate love. There was a longing in days of the altar and the scapegoat for a clearer revealing of God's forgiveness. If only God would walk our streets, bear our shame, and say with lips like ours, "Thy sins be forgiven thee"! [9] When an airplane is wrecked on a mountainside, we wish there could be some radar healing; but the ambulance train must climb by circuitous trails, and doctors must lay hands on broken limbs. There is no radar pardon. If God were to forgive us by some gesture in heaven, how could we know? Albert Schweitzer felt pity for the folk in the Lambaréné Forest before he left Germany, but they were unaware of his compassion until he went to live in the midst of their need.[10] The cleansing of history must be from above history, for only God can forgive; yet it must also be wrought within history, for only so can we know ourselves forgiven.

The next step of faith is now clear: *God coming to earth must suffer.* By necessity of His nature, we surmise, He must suffer; for Holiness must needs be pained by lies. There are no human parallels. An innocent man's pain, when he stands in a police line-up while lights are played on his features and unseen eyes scrutinize him, is no parallel; for there are no innocent men. A mother's agony in the shame of her trusted son is no parallel, for no mother is utterly pure of heart. There are no human symbols of God:

> We may not know, we cannot tell,
> What pains He had to bear; [11]

and Lenten contrition has rightly represented God as saying to His world: "Behold, and see if there be any sorrow like unto my sorrow." [12] By necessity of our nature also, we surmise, God must suffer. In strange but undeniable fact we do not realize the sinfulness of sin until we see its consequence visited upon the relatively innocent. We are indifferent to the hazards of coalmining, and slow to provide safeguards, until a mine disaster opens our eyes. How far this necessity is by God's pristine will, how far by our abuse of freedom and resultant callousness, we do not know. We do know that only tragedy opens our eyes and that tragedy brings what the Greeks called *catharsis*. The cleansing, other factors being equal, is proportionate to the purity of the tragic sufferer. King Lear's grief [13] redeems us more than Macbeth's, for Lear has nobleness. Must we not conclude that ultimate cleansing can come only by the sorrows of God? A further fact holds: the tragic sufferer is himself redeemed by his unaccountable fate if he offers his pain as oblation.

III

If God must come to earth to lay healing hands upon us, what of Jesus Christ? Now we understand His universality, the awe He awakens, His claim and power to forgive, and His abidingness. Surely He is Deity, living with us—and, by the gift of His Spirit, living *in* us—in the joy and pain of persistent love. If God coming to earth must suffer, what of Calvary? Now we understand the strange magnetism of the Cross. That hilltop was fittingly shaped like a skull, for it had been grimly forested with crosses; many had died there before Jesus. Then why is *His* cross remembered, and two others because of His, while all the rest are forgotten? The remembrance is not by man's choice, for man was resolved to blot out all remembrance of Him in the shame of the Cross. Shall we say then that the remembrance chose us? Say rather that Calvary is God's sorrow and therefore our cleansing. Only thus can we find due explanation of the power of the Cross. Rightly an old legend tells that when a rebel against God shot an arrow at the sky, five drops of blood fell from heaven, one from each of the five wounds of Christ. There the sufficient offering for sin was sacrificed, there the ancient Day of Atonement was fulfilled: "Behold the Lamb of God, which taketh away the sin of the world." [14]

Perhaps the Calvary prayer, "Father, forgive them; for they know not what they do," [15] has a deeper meaning than at once appears. It is clear that Jesus there pleads our pathetic ignorance, and that He offers Himself for us, despite our blindest ignorance and blackest sin, in utter and outright love. But perhaps there is an even deeper meaning. Jesus could not pretend that Caiaphas, Pilate, and the unthinking mob were merely ignorant. They were knowingly wicked, and Jesus in His truth offered no excuse for their treachery. Then what is the deeper meaning of "Father, forgive them; for they know not what they

97

do"? Perhaps Jesus meant that the deed of Calvary was beyond man's ken. There God grappled with our sin in the cleansing tragedy of Holiness: "For our sake he made him to be sin who knew no sin." [16] There God gathered all the spears of man's transgression into His own breast. Judas, Caiaphas, and Pilate, though sinful, were still only small-part actors in a drama too vast for their comprehension. Heaven met the power of evil in dread encounter on Calvary, and conquered in love's seeming defeat. How could Pilate and Caiaphas understand that eternal Passion? Yet they could be forgiven: "Father, forgive them; for they know not what they do."

IV

Only God can forgive, yet our response is needed. The pardon is without full effect until man accepts it and lives in its power, as music is null and void until a man opens his ears. The aural nerve is frail, yet without it symphonies are lost. Our first response to the Cross is simply to *expose ourselves* to it. We ask: What manner of man is this who is at home in every land and claims to forgive sins? Why does He quicken reverence by His rigor of truth? Why does He abide? Surely God is in Him! If God is not in Him, it would hardly profit us to be found of God. Why the strange magnetism of His cross? Is this also God in suffering love? What manner of love, stronger even than the ruthless wickedness that slew Him, stronger even than death! Are the same sins in me? Does the same Love seek me? That exposing of the aural nerve to the music of Jesus is the first response to Calvary. A Japanese proverb says, "Forgiving the unrepentent is like drawing pictures on water." [17] So it is, but we can hardly be unrepentant if we keep looking at the Cross.

The next item in response is the simple *acceptance of pardon*. This is hard for human pride. Perhaps it is doubly hard for modern man; for in our generation we have conquered large areas of nature for our physical wellbeing, and are therefore reluctant to admit that we are helpless to save our souls. But how can a man cleanse history? How can a man will to be pure, when the will itself is impure? How can a man repress his remorse when, even if he were to succeed, the repression would work a worse remorse—like a boil plastered down instead of lanced? It is true that we have measurably controlled nature. But it is also true that, because we are unwilling to admit that only God can forgive, our control of nature has been our suicidal undoing. Thus planes become bombing planes. The psychologists wisely tell us that we must learn to forgive ourselves. Self-hate, they say, leads to censoriousness, and thus spreads its wretchedness across the world. But how can a man forgive himself unless he knows that God forgives him? Any other self-pardon would lead only to worse self-hate. The greatest moment comes when we lay aside all pride, plead to be forgiven, and by act of faith in Christ and His cross accept God's pardon. Then we can forgive ourselves, because Christ counts us worthy of His love.

The other item in response is that we should *try to for-*

give. The word *try* is used because human pardon, itself stained with sinfulness, can never show full love. When Friedrich Wilhelm of Prussia was dying, his chaplain bade him forgive his enemies. So the ruler turned to his wife, saying, "Write to your Brother, (unforgiveablest of beings), after I am dead, that I forgave him." The chaplain suggested the message could better be sent without delay. "No," said the monarch, "after I am dead: that will be safer!" [18] Friedrich, ready to forgive, but aware that he might change his mind in a sudden angry remembrance, knew nevertheless that pardon was required of him; for he added, "You do not spare me. It is right. You do your duty like an honest Christian man." God's pardon demands of us in love that we forgive our enemies, as we hope to be forgiven by them. That forgiveness also is renewal of life, not any fiat-word; it is bestowed only by love's pain. God's pardon of our sin gives us strength to forgive, if we will receive it.

V

The taxgatherer, in Christ's parable, freely confessed his sin: "God be merciful to me a sinner." The Pharisee in the same temple at the same hour thanked God that he was "not as other men." [19] Each man's appraisal of himself was true within limits. The Pharisee *was* upright in conduct, faithful in prayer, and generous in gifts; while the publican *was* a "collaborationist" with the Roman conqueror and greedy for gold. But the Pharisee refused to confess his sin and therefore lost sense of nobleness; for only as a man says, "My life is low," can he remain aware of the heights or ever reach them. The publican, on the contrary, had nothing left to his credit except honest confession, but having that he had everything; for that was an open door to God and pardon and eternal life. The Pharisee had everything but the sense of failure, and so had nothing; while the publican had nothing but the sense of failure, and so in God's grace had everything.

God's pardon gives the new motive for life: "We love [Him and our neighbors] because he first loved us." [20] The reformer who sets out to "redeem the world" soon fails, as witness the resentment he provokes, because he is intent on his program rather than on God's forgiving grace. Why do we support the United Nations? Not because *we* can plan wisely for the welfare of the planet, for such wisdom is not given us. Our brief dust cannot read the future, let alone control it. Why then? Because God loved us in Christ; and because as we pray at our juncture in history, asking wisdom in the Holy Spirit, support of the United Nations seems required of us in answering love. We have no world wisdom or world power, still less world redemption. Only Christ can carry the Cross; only God can create and re-create His world. One duty-joy is ours: to live in response to God's love made known in the forgiving grace of Christ. This is our wrestler's hold in the elusiveness of duty, this our grip on the slippery ground of practical wisdom: "Be ye kind one to another, tenderhearted, forgiving one another, even as God for Christ's sake hath forgiven you." [21]

CHAPTER VII

Faith in Life Eternal

"Keep yourselves in the love of God, looking for the mercy of our Lord Jesus Christ unto eternal life."

Jude 21

AN ACTRESS was recently asked her opinion on world politics. Perhaps the reporters assumed, not without provocation, that any opinion, however unversed, would compare favorably with those that have governed world affairs in recent decades. But she answered with no supernal wisdom—she said she expected to be killed by an atomic bomb within five years and proposed meanwhile to have a "good time." "Good" apparently meant night clubs and new clothes—strange way to meet either final death or eternity. But we are all like her in this: the atomic bomb has brought death into the foreground of our thinking. We can no longer hide from death in either business or pleasure. Even the actress will be obliged during her "good time" to remember that five years must swiftly pass. Of any venture nowadays we must add: "If we are still here!"

In one sense the bomb has changed the problem of death: it has printed in heavier type the hyphen that links death and guilt. Profoundly Paul writes: "The sting of death is sin; and the strength of sin is the law." [1] Half consciously everyman knows that death is finality; it ends his chance on earth and sets indelibly the record of his sin. Calvary and Easter are one theme, not two; for if Christ had not been ready to die in holy love, His resurrection could have been no full redemption; and if He had not risen, death would have branded Him a failure. On man's side correspondingly forgiveness and eternal life are one theme, not two; for an unforgiven man might find eternity only an endlessness of his chaotic self, while a forgiven man without eternity would see in pardon only the last meal before the electric chair. Thus the bomb has wrought that change: it is vivid sign of man's sin, or of the demonism to which man has sinfully consented. So the bomb wrings from man the ancient cry: "Sirs, what must I do to be saved?" [2]

But if death *could* be separated from guilt, the bomb has not changed the problem. For a man must die, and dies only once: the problem is the same whether man dies late or soon, by atomic blight or the mumps, singly or in wholesale lots. The problem has to be met, for it waylays us in every obituary column and fatal accident, not to mention war's holocaust. We try to persuade ourselves that death is a natural event, like birth, to be accepted naturally in the order of organic life. But man is not merely organic—he stands above organic life to graph and chart it. John Whale maintains shrewdly that there is a sharp difference between dying and having to die.[3] A cow dies; a man has to die. No Shakespeare cow says, "What a piece of work is cow! how noble in reason! how infinite in faculty! in form and moving how express and admirable!" No Hamlet among cows exclaims: "This goodly frame, the earth, seems to me a sterile promontory." [4] But a man is never at home on the earth. He longs for a better country. He rebels against the apparent finality of death. He yearns for what his eyes cannot see. He has to die. So the universe is brutal, unless—unless there is a heaven, unless a man can live in confident faith of "everlasting life."

I

We pause to prick the balloon which advertises "one world at a time." The pause can hardly be refreshing, but it is necessary; for the balloon fills the modern mind, and there is no climbing over it unless it is punctured. So, sharply: we cannot live in one world at a time, for we are not made that way. A trusted friend dies, and we cannot help wondering about

> The undiscover'd country from whose bourn
> No traveller returns. [5]

That wonder makes us citizens of two worlds, despite our resolve. Perhaps nothing is more childish or pathetic than the modern running away from death. We print the newspaper obituary columns in small type on a back page, hoping thus to persuade ourselves that our name will never appear. We disguise death by the embalmer's art until it seems only sleep, and then say to ourselves, "This is not really death." In Forest Lawn, Glendale, California, sentimental music steals from the trees between funeral services; we spoof ourselves for a brief moment that death is only a lovely trance. Or—favorite escape— we pretend there is no more to us than science laboratories can find, though nobody heard of a laboratory scrutinizing a laboratory.

Therefore, more sharply: scientism, not religion, is the psychological "escape." Business and "a good time," not faith, are the psychological "defense." Christian faith has always been ruthlessly honest about death. It does not sentimentalize. The New Testament does not play "The Londonderry Air" [6] in Forest Lawn. It says in a stab of realism, baring its breast to the dagger, "The last enemy ... is death." [7] So we are to live to make the world a better place? But suppose we cannot greatly improve the world: there are worthy thinkers who assert that there can be no utopia on this planet, because it is only a sketch pad for beginners. Suppose there were a utopia: are the multitudes who have died in pain, looking for the earthly paradise, only fertilizer for that garden? Besides, if utopia should come, would it be any easier to leave? Would not death's mockery then be double mockery?

Advocates of "one world at a time" evade the questions, and no man can live in evasions. Granted that the Church has sometimes mooned about heaven to evade painful duty in a present world, that evasion is still not so unworthy as the evasion of death. What *has* happened to that friend who died? Human nature is at stake: if man is only dust, although intelligent and aesthetic dust, is it worth our while to "make a better world"—of dust? God's nature is at stake: if God uses men as fertilizer, generation after generation, for some brief utopia before the planet disintegrates, is He better than Hitler who used men as cannon fodder for a "new order"? Man is either dust, blown away in the wind of death, or he is a fleshly "bundle of infinity." God is either Hitler, using multitudes in death to build a perfection that is itself doomed, or He is in Christ. The fact of death obliges us to choose a faith —in conduct, if not in creed—or to live teetering between evasions.

We wonder in our best moments if a better world, with its new plumbing, assured wages, and finer schools, really matters. It matters only as a preface; and if the book is nothing but preface, it does not matter. Recently a fine critic asked me bluntly why the Church had failed the labor unions. Unhappily, he had reason to ask. The Church knew, in a day now condemned and passing, that child labor, pittance wages, and slum housing were wrong. But comfortable folk brought pressure on the pulpit, and some preachers failed to speak a clear word. That failure hurt the unions, for it alienated them from Christian faith; it hurt the Church, for it robbed the Church of the witness of brave and compassionate leaders of the cause of the poor; and it hurt the comfortable folk, for unionism, lacking Christian faith, has dealt with the comfortable in narrow bitterness. This I tried to say, and then asked the critic if he thought unionism could be equated with the kingdom of God. Granted wages and hours were a necessary first objective, unions have been slow to see that some work is so mechanized in method and shoddy in product that it is not worth doing at a hundred dollars an hour in a twenty-hour week. I asked also: "Where will it all lead? To death? If to death, is it worth the candle?" Maybe I should have been as blunt as he: "Friend, five minutes after death perhaps neither the C.I.O. nor the Republican Club will cut much of a figure." Doubt of everlasting life can be worthy, for at its best it is inverted faith; and faith can be worthy, for faith far transcends make-believe; but the shallowness of "one world at a time," except it be a protest against sentimentalism in religion, is only an evasion of the questions.

II

Every man believes fitfully or steadily "in the life everlasting." [8] We are so made. If someone were to retort, "Perhaps we are made to doubt," we might have to agree, at least in the admission that faith is never without odds. Some generations, prominently our own, seem beset by doubt; other generations, as in the medieval time, seem prone to believe. But faith is never lost. A man who says, "Life goes swiftly," confesses, however unconsciously, that he has a vantage point above mortality. Napoleon once asked how long a painted portrait would be likely to last. When told that eight hundred years might be the limit, he exclaimed, "Such a poor immortality! I want to live not for eight hundred years, nor for eighty times eight hundred, but forever!" In that issue every man is Napoleon; he yearns for eternal life. Would not stone of a statue also crumble? Then dismiss the sculptor! And call for—whom? [9]

Our faith in eternity is so subtle and overlaid that it is hard to trace and clarify, but it lives. What is the parable? Imagine a man who has never left New York. Some "religious" neighbors tell him that beyond his hard streets there is a countryside. But he travels by the roar of the subway. He is jostled by crowds. He must struggle for livelihood. His nerves are jangled by flash bulbs, sound trucks, and sensational headlines. The city seems almost as hard as its streets—why should he believe in any countryside? Yet at the street corner there is a man with a flower cart, and manifestly flowers do not grow on sidewalks. From Riverside Drive he sees the Hudson, and plainly the Hudson does not rise in New York City. Birds fly into Central Park each spring; there must be some other land. The Narrows give a glimpse of what might be an ocean. The man who has never left New York would always be stumbling on signs to disturb his conviction that there is no other country, as you and I are disturbed when we vow that there is nothing but our mortal life. Whence the flowers of pity if not from some primal garden? Whence the flow of justice which quickens labor movements and overturns tyrannies, unless from some mountain height? Whence the flashing birds of inspiration? And that sight through the Narrows: there are tides too vast to rise in our harbor. Thus modern man cannot escape the faith. As often as he wonders about a friend's death, or protests this world's cruelty, or rebels against the finality of death, he believes, however fitfully, in the life everlasting. If he then prays, his belief is driven deep; and the glow on his mind bears witness that around mortality there is a world of light.

We should not be surprised that the sense of eternity has grown dim in our generation. The Renaissance deserved that name on the surface; there were certain gains. But below the surface the Renaissance may have been retrogression. For men's eyes turned from worship to the world. People began to question rather than to exclaim, to examine rather than to pray. The study of man and nature obtruded as the new foreground, until there was no background. Life became a two-dimensional flatness. Our generation has reached the logical end of the process. Art is now sensate, even to an attempt to capture the moment's swift impression. Learning stresses science— the study of the world, with the senses as method and criteria. Trade is a competitive struggle in which life is eclipsed by livelihood. Success is things. Cities proudly advertise the size of buildings, numbers of population, money wealth and miles of streets. We are dazzled by inventions, as children by new and shiny toys. But weariness has come upon us. Perhaps we shall soon return to the primal springs of life. The deeper struggle in our world is not between old orders and brash revolution, but between man-centeredness and God-centeredness. Meanwhile even our sensate age cannot completely renounce its faith in the life everlasting, for everyman dimly knows another Country.

IV

The resurrection of Jesus Christ meets man's faith as a seed falls into its proper ground. Jesus did not create the hope, for it is world wide and in every man; but Jesus "brought life and immortality to light through the gospel." [10] He saved immortality from being a dreary endlessness, for He brought forgiveness. He gave immortality a new content, richer than this life as this is rich compared with prenatal dimness. He led man's hope from shadows and fears into confidence. This gift began in His words. To the Sadducees, who did not believe in the resurrection from the dead, He spoke of a future incomparably bright: "Ye know not . . . the power of God." [11] To men facing persecution He pledged a Country of the soul: "Do not fear those who kill the body, and after that have no more that they can do." [12] The words were fulfilled in Jesus Himself. A bugle is blown from Castle Rock in Edinburgh at sundown. Once we heard the bugle through heavy fog. We could not see the rock, still less the sunset. But we knew then that there is a rock and a sun's light. How else to describe Jesus? His life is a bugle blown "from the hid battlements of Eternity." [13] His words are like our words, but they have another accent. His deeds are like our deeds, but they are charged with another power. His death is like many another death on our cruel planet, but it cleanses us age on age: we are awe-struck before a Divine pain. By Him we know that, out there above the mist, is the Rock and Sunlight.

The proof of His resurrection is not in what men call proof. We have no record of His voice on Easter Day. If we had, it would not help us; for it would be in a dead language, and any skeptic could still demand, "Prove it *is* the voice of Jesus." We have no affidavit, signed and notarized in the courts, from those who saw Him at the Resurrection. If we had, microscopes would be trained on it, and the skeptic could still pronounce it forgery. These "proofs" would be alien from His mind. He seemed careless of any record. He cast His seed upon the flood. Besides, if Jesus lives, why should He need affidavits or what our literal age calls "proofs"?

Then where do we find the certitude? In the men who testified to His resurrection. They were not predisposed to expect it, and therefore not liable to ascribe objectivity to any mere imagining. Some in Jewry did believe in the resurrection of the dead (the Pharisees, for instance, in contrast with the Sadducees), but a crucified man was reckoned accursed under the Jewish law; and it was a "thing incredible" that such a man should rise as Saviour. So they hardly expected Him to return from that "undiscover'd country": they were not prone in that instance to hallucination. Moreover, they were not gullible men. The New Testament, as anyone who runs may read, constantly warns against self-pretense ("Let no man deceive himself" [14]) and against the pretenses of the world. Furthermore, they were honest men. Those who argue that

111

Paul devised a mystery-cult,[15] and so draped resurrection garments on a comparatively unknown Jewish rabbi, ignore a hundred opposing facts; not least the fact of Paul's insistence that men must be honest for the sake of Christ. Mark his manner of speech: "I say the truth in Christ, I lie not, my conscience also bearing me witness in the Holy Ghost." [16] Of the Resurrection he says flatly that if Christ did not rise from the dead, "then is our preaching vain, and your faith is also vain. Yea, and we are found false witnesses of God." [17] Such deceit horrifies him, even in mere supposition; for Christ is true, and men must be true for His sake. So the certitude of the Resurrection is in the character of the witnesses.

It is also in the nature of the record. One of the earliest accounts is that in the First Letter to the Church at Corinth. It is simple and direct. It exposes itself to scrutiny by summoning many witnesses then alive: "And . . . he was seen of Cephas, then of the twelve: after that, he was seen of about five hundred brethren at once: of whom the greater part remain unto this present, but some are fallen asleep." [18] The words are clear, careful, confident. The Gospels were written at a later date. Even Mark, the earliest Gospel, was penned a full generation after Calvary; and Matthew's Gospel and Luke's were written after two generations. These three writers were not intent on what we call "a historical record." They wrote to transcribe the church's experience of Christ, and thus to confirm the faith of converts and catechumens. We should not expect the resurrection chapters in the Gospels to be written as literal science. Inevitably and desirably they have a literary and confessional cast. But they hold a stanch core of truth, the same core found in the witness to the church at Corinth. Consider the gospel account of the Resurrection. How intimate: "Go . . . tell his disciples and Peter," [19] Peter having denied Him! How instinct with the unexpected: "Jesus himself drew near," [20] the initiative being His in an undreamed-of invasion of love! How lowly: a fabrication surely would have made Him confound the pride of Caiaphas and Pilate, but the Gospels report Him greeting His own with "All hail" [21] and "peace be unto you," [22] the salutations by which friend daily greeted friend! How vital with living experience: the writers knew His very presence!

The certitude of the Resurrection is also in the Church. The New Testament is the witness of a church. There is no "sadness of farewell," [23] but only sunrise confidence. The Order of the Round Table broke when King Arthur died; the Church of Christ came into being when He died—and rose. Disciples who were plunged into gloom by His death under a curse ("We trusted that it had been he which should have redeemed Israel" [24]) suddenly sang hallelujahs and then met an alien world in a faith that knew no fear. The ancient Sabbath became the new Sunday—the day on which He rose. The crucifix became the empty cross of a regnant Lord. That word "seen" in the earliest account of the Resurrection is not amplified. Some New Testament narratives indicate that Jesus rose in flesh; others hint a resurrection body. But behind all

113

accounts is the fact of men who knew that Jesus was with them, not in any frail vision of their minds, but in objective Presence. That knowledge is still instinct in the Church. Only so could the Church live. Even unbelievers thrill to "I know that my Redeemer liveth":[25] such music, they are aware, is not self-bemused. A New York rector recently traced for me, in the graining of the chancel marble in his church, the face of Chirst. I looked and looked, but could not easily see what he saw. Yet I was grateful because of his word and faith; for it would not have occurred to him to say, "There is the face of Christ," if Christ had not been in his heart. Hymns of His nearness are not self-deception; they bring too sharp a condemnation and exact too costly a discipleship. Always He stands at the door: the proof of His resurrection is—His presence.

V

To return to the plea of "one world at a time": those who believe in Christ's resurrection-world have been the best health of *this* world. That fact is a turning of the tables in very truth: the right kind of otherworldliness is the only safeguard of the here-and-now. Admittedly there is the wrong kind of otherworldliness. A father could use music as a lazy trance and so try to justify his failure as breadwinner, but the fault then would be found in the father's selfishness, not in music. Christians who have neglected earth to dream of heaven have not been Christians; they have forsaken Christ to worship

114

comfort. His real followers, believing in heaven, have brought heaven to earth.

Both free enterprise and the labor movement at their best believe in the worth of the individual. But such a faith is nonsense if men are cheap candles blown out at death, or drops of water absorbed into some vague ocean of being. Thus any real faith in personality rests on faith in the life everlasting. Incidentally the phrase "I believe in . . . the resurrection of the body" [26] is intent, not on an exaltation of the flesh, but on personality: the person is value, and will have hereafter, as here, the instruments to express his individual worth. We repeat: only such faith gives meaning to the best crusades of earth. The right kind of otherworldliness is sanity for this world, the saving grace of present duty. John Tauler is an instance. Firmly he believed that Christ "has brought life and immortality to light through the gospel." [27] Therefore he greatly served his day and generation. See him renouncing a money fortune to enter holy orders, thus rebuking money standards not by loud word but by gentle deed; see him choosing three years of silence when fame came upon his preaching, thus bringing silent warning to all human pride; see him cherishing "the Friends of God," thus bringing comradeship into a too-sacerdotal church; see him, in the time of the Black Death, moving through the plague like a ministering angel.[28] Why? Because he believed through the Resurrection in eternal life and the worth of man.

If man is plasticine instead of soul, no "movement"

makes much sense. Man can then be knocked down without reproach in unsafe coal mines, racial prejudice, or periodic war. Totalitarianisms stem directly from the unfaith that man is a mere time organism, a spawn of the economic system. Democracy soon becomes demagoguery, if it loses the credo that man has abiding worth. Only by that positive faith can men find coherence in their life or honor in their God. We should not be misled by cheap gibes about the Bible heaven. Golden streets and pearly gates are easy to parody, but their deep meaning is far nobler than the critic's mind. When men would describe the wonder of life in Christ, they are obliged, by infirmity of mind, to use as symbols the treasures of our present world. Thus "the street of the city was pure gold" [29] means riches unspeakable, in a land without greed. "Harpers harping with their harps" [30] means that earth's wars are resolved in music's most rapturous praise. The "sea of glass mingled with fire" [31] means that tragedy, symbolized (as often for the Hebrews) by an angry sea, is now overpassed; the sea is smooth as a mirror, and the crimson sunset striking into it is token of the fair eternal tomorrow. The "gates" that are "not . . . shut at all by day," and need not be shut at night because there "shall be no night there," [32] means that terror is ended; the blessed live ever in the welcome of God's love. Parody of such adoration condemns itself; the mind that wonders and prays knows "the love of Christ, which passeth knowledge." [33]

VI

Belief in the Resurrection is no comfortable doctrine. It confronts us with a choice. Either we refuse its light for shadows of a mortal cave, or we move from the cave mouth to become explorers of eternity. To dwell in the cave is in some ways easier: the mind can be scientifically compact, and the heart's movements circumscribed in safety. But the shadows deepen into night. To explore eternity is in some ways harder: daylight reveals a vast unknown, and it is not easy in this success-seeking world to live "after the power of an endless life." [34] But the light shines more and more unto the perfect day. Several Easters ago the bookstore at Union Seminary in New York City displayed a number of magazine advertisements. They had one propaganda: they broadly hinted that Easter means shopping for more finery. They pleaded that Easter could not be joyous unless a man bought gadgets or hams or furs. One blurb did mention Christ, but only to claim that the benefit of the Passion music would be gained best through such-and-such a phonograph. The seminary, with fine insight, set beneath the rows of advertisements—a Bible, open at the story of the Resurrection. Belief in the Resurrection confronts us with that choice. Faith in the life everlasting is thus a crux. We can believe one thing or the other about our own life: we are either dust beset by demonism *or* men marked out for a heaven of grace. We can believe one thing or the other about God: He regards mankind as history's fertilizer *or* as His children and the brethren of Christ. To live in the

one choice invites hell; we have seen hell on earth and
ought not to insult one another's intelligence by suggesting there can be no judgment beyond this world. To live
in the other choice is heaven here and hereafter; and the
only way to heaven is through the heaven. "Keep yourselves in the love of God, looking for the mercy of our
Lord Jesus Christ unto eternal life." [35]

SO WE BELIEVE. But faith is fulfilled only in prayer.
Prayer is at once faith's direct act and daily food, faith's
venture and certitude. Faith without prayer is dead.
"Speak to Him thou for He hears." [36] By that speaking
our hand, thrust into the unknown, is found and gripped
by a Hand, and faith becomes certitude. Is there not a
story of a man who saw little to inspire him in Thorvaldsen's statue of Christ, and of a child who said to him, "You
must go close to it, sir. You must *kneel down* and look up
into his face"? [37] Alongside the road of endless argument
and weary seeking there is a postern door that leads direct
to God—the door of childlike prayer. We turn therefore
to the best prayer, the prayer that Jesus taught. SO WE
PRAY.

PART II

So We Pray

CHAPTER VIII

The Lord's Prayer and Our Prayers

"After this manner therefore pray ye: . . ."
Matthew 6:9

TWO SIGNS of Jesus abide, though all else be ignored or forgotten—a prayer and a cross. People who are ignorant about the Bible can recite the Lord's Prayer, and they know that Jesus was crucified. These are His memorial: not a tombstone or a moneyed foundation, but a simple prayer and a gallows set against the daybreak. About five hundred million people say the prayer. If they really prayed it, they could change the world. Napoleon once asked, "Do you wish to see that which is really sublime?" and answered his own question, "Repeat the Lord's Prayer." [1] But apparently that was all he did; he only repeated it. So it left no deep mark on his conduct. But even the man who abuses the Lord's Prayer cannot forget it, and the remembrance is a seed that may yet fructify his barrenness.

I

The Lord's Prayer came in answer to a prayer. The disciples besought Jesus: "Lord, teach us to pray, as John [meaning John the Baptist] also taught his disciples." [2] It was the custom then for a rabbi to give his followers a brief form of prayer, and John had followed the custom. Christ's disciples admitted that they did not know *for what* they should pray. Do we not share their ignorance? My sons when small used to pray their father for knives and matches. We make precisely that blunder, as any war can show—shrapnel-knives and atom-matches! If God wished to be cruel, perhaps He could best succeed by giving us what we ask. "He got what he wanted" usually turns into an epitaph.

The disciples did not know *how* to pray. Perhaps the church seriously fails people in that practical regard. The pulpit urges us to pray, just as it urges us to read the Bible. But the Bible is not easy to understand; and its fuller meaning opens only to those who ask, "Who wrote it? When? Where? Why? How did God speak to him? What does this word require of me?" Likewise prayer is not an easy exercise. It has its own forms, since nothing in mortal life is formless; its own beginning and ending, its own attitude and climate, and a discipline far more rigorous and rewarding even than that of music. Modern man needs this knowledge; it is his prime lack. So long as his earth and his busy fingers have no sky, he must live in a strife-filled prison. The disciples asked to be taught a practical way of prayer; and Jesus, always ready to satisfy a sincere wish, taught them: "After this *manner* therefore pray ye."

II

The Lord's Prayer is both brief and childlike. Pious Jews paused three times each day to pray. The workman would quit his task and the teacher his lesson, to stand before God. That prayer had eighteen petitions.[3] It was three times as long as the Lord's Prayer, which has only seventy-two words in the Greek of Matthew's version and fewer in Luke's version. It is possible, even probable, that the Lukan version more accurately reflects the original prayer, which may have consisted of only three petitions: for the coming of the kingdom, for daily sustenance, and for pardon. The Pharisees, if they could find an admiring audience on a crowded street corner, would pray for three hours in order to build a reputation for piety. Jesus said of them, "They think that they shall be heard for their much speaking." [4] The Ephesians would stand much longer than three hours before the Temple of Diana, crying out in mindless repetition until they almost dropped from weariness, "Great is Diana of the Ephesians!" [5] The prayer wheels of Tibet expose tiny paper prayers, and the devotee turns the wheel all day long.[6] Some of us have known human prayer wheels; they pray interminably in "empty phrases."

Jesus set His face against such unreality. The word "hypocrite" in His warning against babbling prayers could almost be translated "actor": the Pharisee at the street corner was not praying, but only putting on an act. Jesus taught us a brief prayer in terse phrase. Perhaps it was because He knew our human weakness. We find it

123

hard to fix attention for long on anything, and particularly hard in this secular age to fix it on holy things. Once on a train I saw a Roman Catholic priest lay aside his book of required devotions and begin reading *Moby Dick*.[1] That touch of nature made us kin. Perhaps Jesus encouraged brief prayers because He knew that insincerity more easily invades a long prayer. A cry of the heart is staccato. Longing is instant and breaks the bonds of language. So we learn that our prayers can be brief; five hundred words are not necessarily better than fifty. There should be seasons of meditation when we become unaware of the flight of time, but generally the brief prayer is wise—a brief prayer when we rise from sleep, a brief prayer as we meet each joy and challenge of the day, a longer prayer though still brief when we go to bed.

The Lord's Prayer is as childlike as it is brief—childlike, not childish: "Our Father." It does not parade human knowledge, but rather admits an ignorance. It does not pretend to human power, but confesses helplessness: "Deliver us from evil." It pleads no merit, but is acutely aware of human failure and casts itself on Divine grace: "Forgive us our debts." It surrenders all human will to God's will: "*Thy* will, *thy* kingdom, *thy* name." Yet it has awestruck wonder and a glad trust in life's tomorrows: "Thy kingdom come . . . in earth, as it is in heaven." A brief prayer—said slowly, it takes only about thirty seconds. A childlike prayer—it sticks in the throat of a proud man. Understood in the full light of Christ it might be the creed on which all Christians could unite.

III

Yet the prayer is a daring and revolutionary prayer. Jesus was reared in a Jewish heritage, as were His disciples. They had been taught the eighteen petitions of the Shema and that these must be repeated three times each day. Doubtless Jesus did repeat them all His life, and His prayer perfects in both phrase and meaning His nation's best piety; for He came "not . . . to destroy, but to fulfil." [8] Yet it was a daring act to teach His disciples a new prayer. There is a certain imperiousness, set in utter lowliness, not only in His offering a prayer as type and incentive for all our praying, but in the Prayer itself: "After this manner therefore pray ye." His prayer has no novelties; its very phrases are old,[9] rich in the wisdom of man's pilgrimage, more than rich in the ultimate reverences of the soul. But in form and manner the Prayer is still a new song, and its spirit ageless, for He baptized old notes with music's morning dew.

So we find encouragement here to frame new prayers, provided we are true to His model. Probably Matthew's record of the Lord's Prayer is itself a sevenfold form of the original, designed perhaps for the liturgy of the Eucharist, as Luke's record perhaps was so used at baptism.[10] There is virtue in old prayers, and they should not be forgotten. But "new occasions teach new duties." [11] We live, for instance, in an atomic age; mankind has never before traveled this portentous road. Every man, in the invincible loneliness of his inner struggle, daily meets testings which no other man could understand, which indeed he himself does not understand. So we must pray new prayers in new strange times, the Lord's Prayer being still our pattern. Apparently Jesus did not intend it merely for rote: "After this *manner* therefore pray ye." It was to be a seed plot of new prayers. Thus there is a large liberty in this prayer, and a challenge to adventure in prayer; for Jesus might have said, "Except your *prayers* shall exceed the *prayers* of the scribes and Pharisees . . ." If you were asked to go to an airport to break the news of sorrow to a traveler, with only half an hour between planes for the task, you would offer a new prayer; for life would have confronted you with a new task, too taxing for human wisdom, demanding more than human compassion. Yet the Lord's Prayer would still be your guide.

The Lord's Prayer is as revolutionary as it is new. Preachers are sometimes advised to "stick to the gospel," whatever that phrase may mean. It usually means, for people who use it most, that the sermon must move at astronomical distance from daily trade. It means that the preacher should be content to take an anemic Christianity for a Sabbath airing in an ecclesiastical baby buggy. The folly of turning a Christian pulpit into a lecture platform on politics or economics, with accent on the preacher's pet isms, any wise man must admit. But, accepting a phrase at its face value, what would happen if preachers did "stick to the gospel"? A revolution. Our ordinary life would be shaken as by earthquake, and then rebuilt. Take any phrase of this prayer: "Hallowed be thy name";

"Thy will be done." Henry Ward Beecher said that if we really prayed the prayer, "it would make many a man's shop and store tumble to the ground." [12] Should we then quit praying it because we are never fully sincere? No, we should keep on praying it, with thoughtfulness and resolve, until God through the prayer makes us sincere. But we must not try to turn these words into a safe and tepid pietism; they are creative revolution.

IV

The Lord's Prayer gives form to our prayers. A British author has rightly called it "The Model Prayer." [13] It provides an order for prayer, a proper beginning, a rightful sequence, and a true ending. It begins in a name for God. Our finite minds cannot comprehend His glory; we can pray only as we focus on one aspect of His eternal Being. Jesus chooses the central fact, God's love held in wisdom and holiness, and teaches us to begin prayer's adventure in that avowal and trust: "Our Father." Then there is an ascription, "which art in heaven." For we should not break rudely into the Presence, as if we came into the cathedral through the chancel window, but enter quietly through the vestibule of deep reverence. Then come three prayers of adoration and surrender. We are to "seek first" not our covetings, or even our most urgent needs, but God's purpose: "Thy name, thy kingdom, thy will." Perhaps these three petitions correspond to the "Holy, Holy, Holy" of the ancient prayers of Jewry. Almost certainly the description "as in heaven, so on earth"

127

qualifies each, not simply the last, of the three. These three prayers of surrender and adoration are followed by four prayers for our necessities—our daily bread, our need for pardon, our confessed weakness pleading for God's help in the time of testing, our beleaguered soul begging for deliverance from evil. That is to say, the whole gamut of our need is brought before God, from the body's rightful hungers to the soul's defense against the onslaughts of the devil. That sequence of stated need is a progression: the smaller need is for bread, the prime need is for strength and purity of soul.

The word "our" is itself a revolution. No prayer can be selfish, for God is the Father of all mankind. There are no fences of race or class in His eyes: *"Our* Father." "Our daily bread": the bounty of the earth is on one table; all God's children there gather, and the weakest should first be fed. "Our debts": when we pray, we acknowledge our share of the common guilt, and pray God's mercy on our enemy as well as on ourselves. So there is an order of prayer here given, a primacy of adoration, a warranty to bring all our needs to God, a brooding of love that gathers in all mankind. But the heart of the prayer is surrender to God's gracious will and kingdom. The story is told of a man who cut into his weather vane the words, "Thy will be done." Some scoffer asked him if that meant that our obedience is as variable as the wind. "No," the reply came, "it means that whatever the wind or weather we must obey." [14] The Lord's Prayer is undeviatingly Godward, for man is a creature and under authority. The authority is all grace; but even so, man cannot dictate to God or ever turn God's holiness. The Lord's Prayer is glad surrender: "His will is our peace." [15]

The Lord's Prayer links heaven and earth: "in earth as it is in heaven." Whenever we pray it we are joined with loved ones gone from sight. For in that land of clearer seeing they understand, better than we, that God's will is the only joy; and they also pray with surer vision, "Thy will be done, in earth as it is in heaven." Spiritualism is not necessarily false, for no man has right to deny possibility of communication between two realms held in the one Spirit. The condemnation of spiritualism is its drabness: how little its alleged revealings shine with heaven's light! In any event, there is a far better medium of contact than the trances and table-rappings of the mediums —the Prayer in which heaven and earth are joined in one life.

V

Such a prayer is answered, for it was itself an answer to a prayer. The disciples prayed, "Lord, teach us to pray"; Jesus answered the prayer, as God faithfully answers all sincere petitions. The real power in our life is the power of prayer. Almost every word that Jesus used concerning prayer is a word, not of passive resignation, but of dynamic strength: "Ask, seek, knock, find . . . this mountain shall be moved." [16] Almost every word is urgency, not of frantic mind, but of vital fact and immediate need. He spoke as if prayer were the only way of our salvation. There is no "as if"; it *is* the way, the main contact without which the wires and light bulbs of our inventive civilization are mockery. Perhaps an unlit light bulb, ingenious as to filament and glass but still only a dull vacuum, is the cruelly true symbol of a culture that has left no room for prayer. Iron curtains are hung in our world, and man's power is thus made helpless, to reteach us the power of prayer and our dependence on God's grace.

We need not seek any "scientific" proof of prayer's power. There is none, just as there is no "scientific" disproof. Always the answer to prayer can be credited either to "natural causes" or to God. But this (false) alternative confronts us always: violin music is the scraping of horsehair on catgut, or it is—music. If my desk were tidied in a way that humored all my idiosyncrasies, I would say that someone who knows me had been busy for my sake. Over and again life is thus tidied, in startling intimacy of understanding, in answer to prayer; so that a man must exclaim in axiomatic awareness: "This is the Lord's doing; it is marvellous in our eyes." [17]

Likewise we need not covet overt signs that prayer is heard and answered. When we place an infected hand under a doctor's new-ray lamp, we feel no difference. But the next day the infection dies, and the hand begins to heal. So with prayer: whatever we may immediately feel, it does give light at midnight, warmth in winter— and new crusades for our too comfortable souls. "After this manner therefore pray ye"—after how Christlike a manner! Because it is His prayer, it is girded by Him to whom all power is given "in heaven and on earth." [18]

CHAPTER IX

Our Father

"Our Father, which art in heaven."
Matthew 6:9

AN ARTIST who was trying to depict Niagara Falls
threw down his brush in despair. The rainbow wonder
and the majesty of foam defied him. He could as well
hope to paint the unending roar. The Lord's Prayer has
spectrum mists and thunders and powers, and no book
about it can be more than a finger pointing and an awe-
struck voice crying, "See!" Yet the finger and the impoverished voice may yet have their uses in God's grace;
they may persuade someone to confront Him.

As for Niagara Falls, there are people in Buffalo who
say almost casually, even with mild annoyance, "We have
to take visiting friends to see the Falls tomorrow." Fa-
miliarity breeds contempt. It could be so with the Lord's
Prayer. Often we have said it and heard it. Sometimes it
has been gabbled from the pulpit as if it were mere trimming on worship. Rarely is it prayed with trembling and
heart-shaken reverence. Usually people say it rather than
pray it. So we are strangers to the splendor and the power.

Matthew's account suggests that Jesus gave this prayer as a model—"after this manner";[1] Luke's that Jesus intended it as a form—"when ye pray."[2] Perhaps it should be both model and form. Luke tells us that the disciples saw Jesus praying and asked Him then and there to teach them how to pray. They knew, as we know, that mankind is not alone between birth and death, and that we are not meant to live without the Great Companion, and that the power in Jesus was directly traceable to His prayers. So they besought Him: "Lord, teach us to pray."[3] A song is a better memorial than a granite column; a prayer is better even than a song. Jesus lives in this prayer and through it will yet redeem His world. A friend showed me a tiny piece of type metal and assured me that the Lord's Prayer was inscribed on it. The prayer is at home with our littleness, yet no space but only eternity can hold it.

I

It is not true to say that Jesus coined the prayer-name "Father." The title occurs in the Old Testament, though not in prayer. Usually it indicates a national relationship: God was the Father of Israel. Yet there are hints and gleams of a more personal bond, as in the assurance, "Like as a father pitieth his children, so the Lord pitieth them that fear him";[4] and in the intertestamental period, as in the time of Christ, Jewish prayers not infrequently addressed God as Father. Only rarely would a Jew in Jesus' time pray "My Father." This form was deemed appropriate only on the lips of a saint. But Jesus taught blind and sinful men to use it: "Our Father."

That latter fact points a difference between Jesus and His day. For when the Roman prayed "Father Jupiter," or the Greek prayed "Father Zeus," he was using only an honorific name for a god of higher rank in a gallery of gods; and when the Jew prayed "Father" of the one God, the name still had a cast of nationalism, and "Our Father" was the prerogative only of the holy. But Jesus taught all men to pray thus, even men as blind and contentious as His first followers. Moreover—this is the true uniqueness of the prayer—He made the title sovereign, regulative, and redemptively intimate. The aloneness of the title does not come from startling novelty, for the word Father in prayer was not novel; and if it had been novel, it would have been bafflement rather than guidance. The aloneness comes from centrality of emphasis and newness of content, and from the fact that He taught you and me, though we are weak and wicked, to use the word. When we do use it in sincerity, a door is opened through which God Himself finds us in holy love. God is Father, mankind is a family; and, said Jesus in effect, the pattern of society in trade or politics or church must become that of a home.

We need not be ambushed by the critic's gibe: "Anthropomorphism!" Admittedly Father is a human word applied to God. But we have no words that are not human. We cannot leap out of our finitude to declaim in some angel tongue. Perhaps the proper answer to the sneer that an ox would regard God as a larger ox is "Of course." The critic himself speaks of the laws of the cosmos, thus attributing to the universe, at least partially, the patterns of his own mind. This could be called legomorphism; and, we might add, there would seem to be less sense in comparing God with a law than with a man, for laws imply personal will. Besides, no human thinking is *merely* anthropomorphic, for we are always aware of a beyond, a hinterland of mystery:

> Thoughts hardly to be packed
> Into a narrow act,
> Fancies that broke thro' language and escaped.[5]

That beyond is acknowledged when we say "which art in heaven." Thus the anthropomorphism, though inevitable, is set in a confessed Mystery and thereby saved from its narrowness. We have right to compare God with our best. Indeed we have more than right; we have obligation, and the further obligation to admit (what we deeply know) that our best but hints a glory that is beyond our thought. Our best, so Jesus taught us, is a righteous and loving home.

II

"Our Father": the word means *authority*. The title as Jesus used it grew in Jewish soil, even though in Him the flower had universal fragrance; and Judaism was a patriarchal culture. We find a moving instance of that fact in the Passover meal. The father as acknowledged head of the home recounted the story of Israel's redemption in the safe crossing of the Red Sea; the father presided at the feast; the father blessed the unleavened bread and the chalice. Thus the title "Our Father," far from hinting any easy indulgence, spells out a sovereignty, even though it be a sovereignty of love. It is worlds removed from the modern cheapness or rebellion that casually dismisses "my old man." It requires of those who use it an obedient devotion.

The authority is not usurped in any age. Contour plowing is a sermon, for there God in the land says, "You shall honor my hills and valleys for your good; or your soil, which is really My soil, shall run away down every hillside stream, and you shall lack bread." The Exclusion act [6] which barred the Japanese from our shores was a sharper sermon: God taught us in the consequences that there can be no final exclusions in the family of mankind, for exclusions breed hatreds, and hatreds breed wars, and the family can survive only in obedience to the God and Father of mankind. Our pride tries to break the sovereignty but succeeds only in breaking itself. We are creatures. We can become creators only as we are first creatures. Wise men accept this truth, and then discover in lowliness that the truth is a friend.

We are prone to argue that the fatherhood of God when it is construed as sovereignty is not democratic. Perhaps a keener mind would see that only so can any democracy abide. Even in a human family there can be no complete equality; mother and babe are not scientifically equal. Parenthood, if only because parents have experience and children are born in weakness, must exercise wise and loving control. Besides, a democracy that regards each individual man as a final court of appeal will fracture into a million belligerent splinters. Only as each man knows within himself one and the same sovereign Will can the "rule of the people" be better than Babel. Each ship on an ocean has a certain liberty, such as God gives to each man; but the liberty would make the ocean ways a shambles if each ship did not take its bearings from the skies and then obey the rules of navigation. Besides, is it not true that we all deeply desire not democracy but discipline? "His will is our peace." [7] If we desire democracy, as we ought, it is democracy within that deeper bond. The sovereignty is thus our best yearning. Our life is satisfied only in that fealty.

III

"Our Father": the word means not only authority, but *holiness*. This is implied in "which art in heaven." The exact translation is "which art in the heavens." That realm, so people then believed, was separated from earth by a firmament filled with water:

> that inverted Bowl we call The Sky,
> Whereunder crawling coop't we live and die.[8]

Later Jewish thought was fond of dividing the heavens into seven different strata, the "seventh heaven" being God's dwelling place. Job veils his eyes before the holiness of God as he writes: "Behold, he putteth no trust in his saints; yea, the heavens are not clean in his sight." [9] According to Christian thought, Christ descended from the heavens, and there the redeemed shall dwell. The very word heavens breathes holiness. Jewish reverence shrank from speaking the Divine Name; so holy is He that men must approach Him from afar, in such phrases as "which art in heaven."

Thus the prayer "Our Father which art in heaven" invites the refining flame of Holiness. The money standard of success, whether for men or nations, has no chance in that fire. Man does not set the standards; they are in the holiness of God: "Ye shall be holy; for I am holy," [10] saith the Lord. That is why greed capsules a man and makes wars. "Our Father" opens the door to Holiness to be our guest. So there is no indulgence in the prayer. It is foolish for us to assume that judgment will by-pass us while we reckon it irrevocable for our neighbors, for no man can escape God. In *The Rubáiyát* the pots discuss the Potter, as we discuss God. One scorned his Creator: "Who *is* the Potter, pray?" Another scorned his own life: "He . . . should stamp me back to common Earth again." Another spoke in our cavalier mood:

> Folks of a surly Tapster tell,
> And daub his Visage with the Smoke of Hell;
> They talk of some strict Testing of us—Pish!
> He's a Good Fellow, and 'twill all be well.[11]

God is not daubed with any vindictive "smoke"; but the title "Our Father" spells no indulgence, and there *is* "some strict testing of us." The reason that the universe cannot keep a secret, that "what is heard in the ear" shall be "proclaimed upon the housetops," [12] is God's holiness. His light penetrates, consumes the dross in us, and heals.

IV

"Our Father": the title is yet *all love*. Man whose days are more brittle than fine-spun glass may pray to Him whose power moves the stars through ages: "Our Father." Man whose deeds are stained with folly may pray to the Sovereign Will before whom even angels are not blameless: "Our Father." That such a prayer should have been given by Jesus Christ and understood by blundering men is a miracle; for it is the assurance that we, despite the devil's wiles and our weak acquiescence, are yet in some hidden center made in the image of God. God's authority stands eternal, but is yet for our good. God's holiness shines inexorably as light, but is yet intent upon our joy. Nothing need dismay us, for we have "our Father." His authority is not broken, His holiness cannot misconceive our well-being; and authority and holiness are the diastole and systole of His heart of love.

Why are we born? Because Love must bring forth children—to live in Love's devotion. Why is the earth filled with beauty and bounty, and with such singular accord as that between eye and earth and sun? Because fatherly concern has built the house and spread the table. Why is necessity of toil laid upon us so that we must daily win our livelihood from our friend-enemy, the cosmos? Because children grow under responsible endeavor. Why have the means of travel compressed the world into one neighborhood? Because Hands are round about us constraining us into family nearness. Why are we stricken by remorse when we violate our conscience? Because the holy love of God thus moves in us, and His grief thus revealed shows us that we are made, not for sinning, but for sainthood.

Why pain? The very question aches and finds no easy answer. There is enough pain on earth to make any man despair; or, rather, there would be enough, if man's awareness of God were not stronger in all the generations than his awareness of pain. Pain of itself is the servant of death, as any tortured face or racked body can show. But pain made an oblation to God, a strange and bitter offering, becomes, beyond any easy moralizing or pious cant, the servant of life. For Beethoven's music grew to thunderous praise when it was wrung from his deafness, and Tennyson's poetry became apocalypse when he dipped his pen in tears.[13] Why must man suffer the inexplicable yoke of pain? There is no logical answer. We should flee the man who in brash and shallow mind presumes to peddle a "simple solution" to the "problem of pain." Yet earthly parents thrust their children into cold water to teach them to swim, and expose them to the politics of grade school to encourage their growth. We are but children. Therefore we do not know why we should go through this school of life or ever travel the dark valley; but those who have prayed "our Father," and ventured on the prayer, have not lacked secret tidings that all is well. They have been persuaded that pain and death are also His angels.

V

"Our Father": we ought not to slide over the pronoun. The whole Church is in the word "our." As the Church prays in intercession, the whole family of nations is in it, and every least child of man. Despite the book title *Live Alone and Like It*,[14] such a venture would be doomed. For nobody can live alone, much less like it. Every art practiced by a hermit was learned from the common life. An utterly lonely man would soon doubt his eyes and ears, for the guarantee of our senses is in our neighbor's jocular phrase: "Do you see what I see?" But even before such a doubt could spread, the utterly lonely man would have died, for the paradox of his nature demands community while it must keep selfhood. Incidentally, the fine authoress of the book above mentioned was soon afterward married.

In prayer also we are both individual and social. For a man to assert that he can be Christian without the Church is as foolish as to pretend that an arm could live without its body. There is no hermit music, for even a solo implies a composer, just as he implies a long list of prior composers; and a soloist would die of sadness if there were no one to listen. How could Christ ever teach or live a hermit faith? The Lord's Prayer reminds us in its very first word that God is intent, not merely on individual perfection, but on the Beloved Community.[15] It is true that corporate prayer would grow thin if each man did not pray in secret; but it is also true that lonely prayer would die of loneliness, and perhaps of lovelessness, if it knew no social bond.

"Our": in that word all the barriers are down. A small boy asked his father as they walked through Harlem: "Are they really different from us?" They are not different; they with us are born for adoption as the "sons of God." Another child asked: "Why are there so many poor people in the world?" That question, like the other, is a bomb to blow up smugness. There are "so many poor people" because the "haves" forget that they and the "have-nots" are children of one Father. Lines of economic creed find no place in the love of the Lord's Prayer. The white-collar group and the labor union and the manufacturers' association are here all one; they are children of one family, even though they may be quarreling children. National fences likewise are removed, except in the small height needed to make good neighbors. There are no enemy aliens in this temple; every man is a member of the family. Charles Dickens says of Christmas that it shows us to be friends, not "another race of creatures bound on other journeys." [16] But Christmas and Easter both stem from Christ; and men become one, not in a feast day, but only in His spirit who taught us to pray, "Our Father." How can there be brotherhood without a Fatherhood? The word brotherhood cries out for God, and any crusade for brotherhood is homeless and bereft except at the place of prayer.

VI

Thus the first two words of the Lord's Prayer bring us under the sovereignty of God, expose us to the fires of His holiness, hold us in His love—and at the same time bind us in a family bond with every child of man. If we really understood these two words, we might have neither wish nor need to go beyond them; "all this, and heaven too" [17] is enough even for the yearning soul.

It is true that "to labor is to pray," as Benedict taught his order;[18] but that motto finds its life only in another in which the words are reversed: "To pray is to labor." We must eat and rest before we can work, as the activism of our times is slow to learn; and perhaps we should therefore retort to Jean Paul F. Richter's "Only deeds give strength to life" [19] that only prayer gives strength to deeds. "They that wait upon the Lord shall renew their strength." [20]

Who dares to pray this prayer? No one should dare in his own right, but everyone may at the invitation and guarantee of Jesus Christ. In His pain we see the meaning of pain. In His cross we are apprehended by the seeking love of the Father. Only He who had no need to pray "Forgive us our debts" could teach us thus to pray; for "God was in Christ, reconciling the world unto himself." [21] In His name we may make the great venture, daring the invisible: "Our Father." For Marc Antoine Muret spoke truth in his famous answer. The doctors thought him as ignorant as he was poor: *"Faciamus experimentum in anima vili"* ("Let us experiment upon the worthless animal"). He replied in Latin as good as theirs: *"Vilem animam appellas pro qua Christus non dedignatus est mori"* ("You call one worthless for whom Christ did not refuse to die").[22] Christ validates the prayer: "Our Father." The proof of the prayer is in the prayer itself. Try it, and see.

CHAPTER X

The Hallowed Name

"Hallowed be thy name."

Matthew 6:9

OUR DAILY SPEECH is filled with word patterns, phrases that slide from the tongue with hardly more meaning than their sound. We meet a friend and say, "How do you do?" but hurry on our way before he has a chance to tell us. Actually we do not wish to know how he does; the phrase has become a word pattern for a casual friendliness. Or we say "Good-by," which is a contraction of "God be with you"; but, far from meaning it, we may not even know what it means. Word patterns infest political speaking; when a congressman begins to declaim about "this gre-a-a-t nation," we can be sure that he is getting drunk on phrases, and that his discourse on "freedom" will blindly ignore the fact that man the creature can have no freedom except within a preordained orbit. Even college presidents are beguiled by empty phrases: "What we need is more education"—education being undefined, with no account taken of the unfortunate truth that an educated crook is even worse than a crook. As for luncheon clubs, clichés about economics are staple diet.

The Church, paying frequent visits to these glass houses, has no license to throw stones; for word patterns have invaded our prayers. The original imprint on the great terms of Christian theology has worn so thin that this precious coin is now poor currency. "Hallowed be thy name": do we mean it? Do we know what it means? Gerald Heard has written that the petitions of the Lord's Prayer are as "laconic as a chemical formula for making dynamite." [1] Perhaps "as vital as wheat seed" would be a a better simile. Whatever the figure of speech, the Lord's Prayer breaks through our ordered selfishness. If we really prayed it, we would find ourselves saying, "Lord, break me and remake me."

I

The startling implications of "Hallowed be thy name" are not far to seek. This implication is clear: the world is a pagan world. Otherwise there would be no occasion for the prayer. The opposite of "hallowed" is "profaned." Jesus would not have taught the prayer if mankind had not been guilty of profanation. The mood of this prayer is "Holy, holy, holy, is the Lord of hosts"; [2] but our trade and politics, our art and our worship, are far from being "young-eyed cherubim" choiring the Eternal Mystery. We do not stand in awe; we "know it all." We doubt God and deny Him; or rather, we doubt Him in our arguments mainly because we deny Him in our life. If we have any

God, we are our own god; or we worship "progress," by which we mean gadgets, though gadgets have become our tools of wholesale death. Jesus was a realist; He knew that the City of Mansoul[3] is a profane city, and He grieved over our paganism. Therefore He bade us pray that this planet may be redeemed into a Sanctus: "Hallowed be thy name."

Another implication is clear: God Himself must do the hallowing, for profane men cannot of themselves work a holy change. New York City has lately engaged in cloud-seeding to make rain. Even if the result were certain, or better than scanty, there is presumably only a certain total volume of rain; and what one locality takes, another loses. But such considerations aside, how would we fare if there were no clouds, if we were obliged to trust to such synthetic H_2O as we might manufacture? We would die. Carry that helplessness into the far more difficult climate of man's spirit. There we are doubly helpless; we cannot contrive the healing rain of holiness. The truth that only God can save us is scored deep on our present impasse. The passive form of "hallowed be" really means the active form "hallow." The passive is used only because a man must be slow to speak to God in the imperative mood. This prayer is veiled command, the command being wrung from bitter need that only God can fill: "Hallow Thy name!"

There is a still deeper implication. It is hidden in the future-looking tense of the verb and in the thought forms of that age. Scholars tell us that Jesus' teaching has an "eschatological" stamp. Men then believed that history would soon come to a climax, and the mind of Jesus was not alien from that belief. Greek thought in general regarded the story of our world as cyclic: history repeats, the "music goes round and round," and there is nothing new under the sun. Modern man deems life an evolution. The word has almost victimized us. We take a surface development traceable in biology and botany, and print it without warrant on man's body and soul. As for our body, there is little evolution in the fact of death; and as for our soul, the twentieth century could hardly pose as exhibit of evolving saintliness. Perhaps there is no progress on the horizontal line of history. Perhaps the vital line is vertical, the line from God to man, the line of prayer that cries, "Hallowed be thy name." We begin to see that Jesus and His earliest followers, though they foreshortened history to bring culmination near—He perchance in instant vision, they in a hope bred in persecution—had the right world view. Is the planet disintegrating by radioactivity, as science suggests, into a coldness that cannot support life? Will man's folly hasten the end? Is our individual death a symbol of world death? This much is clear: space-time appears to be infected with transience. There is no necessary permanence in history. We must deal honestly with the eschatological cast of the Lord's Prayer. What this petition really means is: "In our pagan realm, in our helplessness, make Thy Name holy in the judgments of the final consummation!" Such is the prayer that we have turned into a casual word pattern.

II

This strange treasure being hidden in the verb "hallow," what of the noun "name"? "What's in a name?" Almost everything so far as the Bible is concerned, for the Bible might almost be called a Book of names. There is not much meaning in our names. "Edgar" means a javelin to protect property, though few Edgars own a javelin, and most of them no real estate. "Irene" means peace, but the meaning can hardly be true or our thousands of Irenes would have overcome our wars. As for our surnames, they have been so changed by the years that they are now only a tag by which the mailman marks us off from our neighbors. But the Bible gathers around names for God, each of them ultimate in meaning. For God's "name" means God's nature shown in God's own acts. Therefore the commandment: "Thou shalt not take the name of the Lord thy God in vain: for the Lord will not hold him guiltless that taketh his name in vain." [4]

God's name is revealed in His creation act. Call it intimate power. Flames leap from our sun a half million miles into space, but the light suits our eyes and brightens our homes. There is power enough in a sack of soybeans to destroy the planet, but drugs enough to work a miracle of healing. It is true that nature is cruel, with tornadoes and tidal waves and blights; or, rather, would be cruel if our body were the last word. So let us say that there is cruelty enough to remind us of the "fear" of the Lord, of the Mystery which we cannot fathom but which yet provokes our worship, of a terrible Goodness that does not go our sentimental or pedestrian pace. Thus God's name is written in the cosmos in kindliness, fidelity, pleading loveliness, yet in saving terror.

God's name is written in human story, like a recurring phrase on a palimpsest, in flash and gleam rather than in unmistakable word. Thrones in His sight are a bauble, and empires are leaves driven on the wind; while meekness, deceptive in its frailty, abides. His law is inscribed on every heart. That is why mankind drafts laws. The story of Moses and his commandments cut into stone is dismissed nowadays as "folklore"; but commandments are always heard on a mountaintop where man meets God, man with open face and God with veiled face, amid thunders and lightnings, and the laws thus given are more enduring than rock. No man breaks them, though he may break himself on them; they are from the foundation of the world. Always some truth troubles man; always he is cursed when he rebels, and blessed when he obeys. Again there is mystery, for no human mind can see history except as a palimpsest; but sober minds can see light and darkness glinting through it, and reverent minds can catch phrases of the song which seraphim chant eternally around the Throne: "Holy, holy, holy, is the Lord of hosts."

God's name is written in Jesus. It would little avail to ask how we know. That would be like asking how we know that Beethoven's "Hymn to Joy" is joyous. If a man were to say, "It is not joyous to me," he would not condemn the music; he would tell only his own morbidness.

149

There is no logic to establish an axiom, for an axiom is the basis of all logic; and the soul of Jesus has axiomatic truth. Jesus is light, and there is no proof for light except light itself. It would be mild folly to ask why Jesus should thus be singled out from all men. For He was not singled out: His foes killed Him lest He be singled out, and His friends took flight. He has right to say: "Ye have not chosen me, but I have chosen you." [5] We never quite escape Him, for He is now in the longing of our world, as life-giving oxygen is in air. One sentence in the palimpsest is clear and in letters of gold: "God hath sent forth the Spirit of his Son into your hearts, crying, Abba, Father." [6] Nature and history alike receive interpretation through Christ; otherwise they are garbled pages. The Father is known through the Son: "He that hath seen me hath seen the Father." [7] So the first petition of the Lord's Prayer means "Hallowed be thy name" of *Father* made known in Jesus Christ. The name of God is the nature of God revealed in God's own acts, and supremely in the seminal and final act of the Incarnation.

III

Thus this first petition does not mean "Make Thy name holy," for God's name is always holy. It does not mean "Reveal Thy name as holy," for that revelation is already given. It means "Hasten the climax of history when all must see, when earth's cheapness shall be shriveled in judgment flame and earth shall chant with heaven: 'Holy, Holy, Holy.'" Subsequent petitions in the Prayer are pendant on this prayer. All the praying man can do is to pray the prayer, prepare for its certain answer, and persuade other men to that same preparation.

Dr. Clarence Edward Macartney, in his book *The Lord's Prayer*,[8] has laid stress on one important item in this preparation: namely, a guard upon our lips that our speech may be hallowed. Profanity of tongue is so widespread in our time as to be almost unconscious. A blasphemous man has been known to apologize in presence of a minister or priest. Perhaps it is a ludicrous apology, for the blasphemer's primary dealing is not with any ordained or unordained neighbor, but with God. Perhaps it would be ludicrous for the man to apologize to God, for the attempt to insult God is like trying to blacken the sky with a tarbrush: the vandal does not hurt the sky, but gets the tar on himself. What is required of him then is no glib apology to man or God, but a plea for God to cleanse the stain: "Hallowed be thy name." Words are not only the issue of a man's soul, but by reflex the fashioner of his soul. Dr. Macartney's plea has urgency and, nowadays, timeliness. An age that is foully or flippantly irreverent in speech has only foulness and flippancy in store —that, and the Judgment.

Dr. Ernest Fremont Tittle, in his book also entitled *The Lord's Prayer*,[9] chooses for his stress another item of preparedness: namely, the resolve on holiness in our common life. He also writes with sharp verity. The Tory, he says, prays "Hallowed be thy name," but then opposes all change, though injustice is plainly rife. The militarist prays "Hallowed be thy name," and then, whatever be his verbal and protested faith, trusts in brute force; and, though force in our world is plainly competitive, step by step from bows and arrows to H-bombs to another dark age, still he trusts in force. The Pharisee prays "Hallowed be thy name," but actually believes in his own arid righteousness and his recited creeds of prejudice. Who could doubt that Dr. Tittle has written with the penpoint of truth? Always we are in danger of exalting our name when we think we are hallowing God's name. Gerald Heard has reminded us of a story in this regard—of the child who thought the prayer was for her and her name, and who therefore said "Halliwell be thy name"; and who felt, when she visited a friend and neighbor, that courtesy required her to substitute the host's name and so revised the prayer: "Cabot be thy name." [10] We are not unlike that child. Subtly we set our big battalions or our theory that prayer is only autosuggestion or our "progress" in the place of the name of God.

But the central preparedness is not in purity of speech or justice in the common life, but simply in the prayer itself. When a man keeps praying the prayer, knowing what it means, his speech will be purified, and he will not sell out to any of the group hankerings that now disfigure society. The prayer itself is so staccato, so wrung from the heart, that it is almost an SOS. The main issue is not circumspection of speech, for the saints have not always been circumspect. The main issue is not the pattern of our common life, for socialism can deify the average man or invite the demagogue. The main issue is that we should dare to pray the prayer, and keep on praying: "Lord, end all our paganisms in Thy judgment, and cause the wrath of men to praise Thee." That heartfelt prayer calls down God's power on our helplessness, and burns away our dross—in capitalism and in unionism, in politics and in art, in speech and in statecraft; and, by holy fire, in the life of the Church.

IV

We should be slow to ask what the prayer can do for us. That would be like asking what use there is in daffodils, or stars, or the martyrdom of Jan Hus. No use, except the coming of God. This prayer purges the word "use" of its own profanations and then fills it with tender ministries, just as Gounod's "Sanctus" sung only as worship then brings healing to the singer. The other day in a church, while the choir sang "Holy Art Thou" to the massive chords of Handel's "Largo," a minister came down the aisle, half an hour late for worship, caught sight of a friend at the end of a pew, and shook his hand. An observer, even from the distance of his seat in the chancel, could almost hear him say: "Hi, Bill, old scout!" Perhaps he is a symbol. Perhaps he is our whole generation. Perhaps there are organ harmonies and angel choirs to which we are deaf. Perhaps we wander blasphemously down the aisle of God's world, pushing a huckster's cart, arguing our isms, or toting a gun, where we should be awe-struck. Sir Christopher Wren gave instruction, when St. Paul's

Cathedral was being built, that any workman heard swearing on the job would be dismissed.[11] There are signs that our generation *has* been dismissed and will starve until it returns with the prayer "Hallowed be thy name."

What can this prayer do? It is the air pipe by which we live, we who are divers moving through the dim light of our subterranean world. The rapture of worship and the vision granted by the prayer are moments when we come to the surface to breathe the air of an eternal kingdom. On earth we grope in half-shadows, not understanding the real world, but not fearing it if through prayer we have found that there is a Friend at the other end of the line. The Sanctus of our prayer is born of the Sanctus in heaven, however poor the echo: "Holy, holy, holy, is the Lord of hosts."[12] These lines are written that the reader may prepare for life permanently above the surface, and that heaven's light may be joy and not pain. "Hallowed be thy name."

CHAPTER XI

The Coming of the Kingdom

"Thy kingdom come."

Matthew 6:10

WE DO NOT LIKE the word kingdom; it savors of totalitarianism. History has given reason for the distaste, for the charter of freedom has been won from kings at bitter cost, all the way from King John to Hitler. But on the rebound from the word kingdom, we are in danger of so deifying the word democracy that each man "dubs his dreary brethren Kings." [1] For if every man is his own judge, demagoguery is just around the corner; and the demagogue is only a cruel king by another name. Even politicians have sense enough to see that democracy cannot live without "standards." But the politician, being interested in votes rather than in etymology, does not know that the word standard is derived through the French word for banner—the banner of God which waves above every man's life to save democracy from chaos. So the word kingdom, though it may threaten death when applied to men, is the promise of life when used of God. Besides, kingdom in the Lord's Prayer is the Father's kingdom.

Judaism believed profoundly in the kingdom of God. Old Testament thought, whether in contrition or praise, never long forgot that royal banner: "Thy kingdom is an everlasting kingdom, and thy dominion endureth throughout all generations." [2] Israel was a buffer state in the midst of ambitious empires, so it was not strange that "kingdom" for the Jew gathered a nationalistic color; he believed that God would establish His reign through the exaltation of Israel. Thence the emphasis on the keeping of the law; for to the Jew the law was the yoke of the kingdom, and the pious believed that if the chosen people would keep only two Sabbaths in perfect obedience, the kingdom would come.

The word kingdom as used by the men of Jesus' time was thus freighted with meanings, some good and some bad. All masterwords, such as the word democracy, suffer that adulteration; and a wise democracy will keep a purifying plant for its master words. How did Jesus use the word kingdom? That is a leading question, for until it is answered the second petition of the Lord's Prayer cannot be understood. In Matthew's Gospel the phrase "kingdom of heaven" occurs thirty-two times, and the more personalized "kingdom of God" four or five times. In most of these instances Jesus is the speaker. The historic creeds hardly mention the kingdom, but for Jesus it was sun by day and star by night Then for Him kingdom meant what? Let us answer provisionally that He lived in its light, and that its light lived in Him, and that the central and sufficient interpretation of the Lord's Prayer can be found only in the Lord Himself.

I

"Thy kingdom come" means that *the kingdom has already come*. For we could not pray the prayer, or even make sense out of it, unless the kingdom had already reached the outposts of our life. The prayer would be nonsense if the kingdom were not already in our ken. "As in heaven, so on earth" probably attaches all three first petitions in the Lord's Prayer. Certainly it belongs to all three by implication. Again the presupposition is that we are aware of "heaven."

> Not only around our infancy
> Doth heaven with all its splendors lie.[3]

Fitfully through all our years we see His banners above our city walls. Our sins are our resistance to His gracious siege, in the foolish fear that we would lose everything in that surrender. No man but can say:

> I dimly guess what Time in mists confounds;
> Yet ever and anon a trumpet sounds
> From the hid battlements of Eternity;[4]

and in that sense the kingdom has already come.

The natural scientist traces the kingdom's laws in the cosmos: the precision of the stars is the sign of a sovereign order. The medical scientist traces the kingdom's laws in our physical body, and tells us that we are healed by obedience, and knows that he, the doctor, is but a servant of the kingdom. The psychiatrist traces the kingdom's laws in our mind; not yet is he ready to use kingdom language, but more and more he speaks kingdom truth, for "confidence" in life is nothing unless it is confidence in the hidden and encompassing Realm. The social scientist traces the kingdom's laws in our common life, the main law being that the good of one is the good of all; and—who knows?—the social scientist may one day confess that mysterious "good" is God. Under the stress of our apocalyptic times many a sober-minded man has become a prophet. He knows there is Dominion round about us which decrees that individual greed grinding the faces of the poor or national greed coveting power is never with impunity, but results in wars that leave us aghast: "It is a fearful thing to fall into the hands of the living God." [5]

The kingdom has already come. We see its banners above our barricades. We know that our freedoms are only by sufferance, or, rather, that the gracious King is a Father who would rather His reign were by our choice than by His compulsion. In the consecration service for bishops in the primitive church, the bishop-elect was exhorted to remember eternity; and recently at such a service in Canterbury Cathedral the old custom was kept, for, as the new bishop passed through the midst of the people, they cried to him: "Remember eternity! Remember eternity!" [6] Actually no man forgets, or can forget. As often as he concludes his prayers "forever and ever," he remembers eternity; and as often as, from city suburbs that try to blink the fact of poverty, he is troubled in conscience, he remembers eternity. The kingdom is always beating at our unavailing walls. The kingdom has already come. It is there, no further than the gates, with spies already in the city. So we pray "Thy kingdom come."

II

But *the kingdom has not yet come,* or there would be no need to pray the prayer. The City of Mansoul,[7] having been granted a limited freedom, still defends its walls against the radiant siege. The kingdom has not yet come in you or me. If proof were needed, it could be found in the fact that we condemn widespread evils without blaming ourselves. No generation has been shrewder than ours in tracing social ills, but perhaps none has been more reluctant to cry, "God be merciful to me the sinner." [8] The psychologists remind us that denunciation is often a "transfer": we try to shift blame on our neighbors to avoid pain of confession. Communism can easily be made a scapegoat. That it is earthy and blind is plain to see; in its ethical relativisms it could become Antichrist. But we shall never really cope with it until we ask, "Whence and why?" The First World War gave it a start, and the Second World War spread it, because communism thrives on man's misery rather than on Marx's dubious ideology. So the partial answer to "Whence and why?" is that comfortable people, such as you and I, have not greatly cared that other people lived in misery. Thus communism, at least in some measure of blame, is back on each bourgeois doorstep. The kingdom has not come in you and me.

It follows that the kingdom has not come in our corporate life, for the word "you" or "I" is not hermetically sealed. The hyphen in social-individual is an unbreakable bond. Each of us lives on a road, not in hermit solitude. Means of communication have now turned the world into one short and crowded street. Our denunciations of world ills, though they are easily made a "transfer," are still more than cogent. Governments in a democracy are perhaps no worse than any average man, for people elect those who govern; but governments can and do become hierarchies of rebellion. They organize the small letters of individual wrong into the capital-letter phrases of public guilt. Dr. J. E. Roberts has thus written blunt truth: "The coming of the kingdom would mean the death of flunkeyism . . . in the personal life, the death of mammon in the social life, and the death of jingoism in the national life." [9] The prayer "Thy kingdom come," if only we knew, is asking God to conduct a major operation. How much the coming kingdom would cut away from the body social becomes clear by only five minutes of scrutiny. That product advertised on the air is instance of the need for the scalpel. Let the reader choose the product in secret—the writer does not covet any drab and sudden death. Would the kingdom's light allow the product to be hawked after news of disaster: "Fifty persons died in the plane crash, and now a word from our sponsor"? By kingdom laws is it right to "triple our sales" by ballyhoo, when presumably there is an inevitable ceiling on sales, and what one man gains another must lose? By the kingdom test does competitive advertising make final sense, each product increasing advertising to increase sales, each roadside a disfigurement, each radio a Babel of hucksters, until the advertising vine kills the tree?

So the kingdom has not yet come. The prayer is mingled certitude and penitence—certitude because we know the banners are just beyond our walls, and penitence because we are equally aware that the City of Mansoul is in rebellion against the King. Dr. J. D. Jones in this connection draws the distinction known in law between a claim *de jure* and a claim *de facto*.[10] The illustration helps our understanding of the prayer: God has holy and loving claim to rule, but in this planet the rule is not in effect. But we must not press the distinction too far, for no man rebels with impunity; and in that sense the kingdom has already come. There are no parables for God's dealings with us. But—it is a poor picture—when I preside godlike over our domestic tank of tropical fish, allowing the zebra fish and the rosy barbs and the angel fish to swim through the tiny castle arch and among the weed as each fish may choose, could any fish rightly say that my rule is only *de jure*? If a fish becomes diseased, I say, "Out of there!" and consign him temporarily to a smaller, unwelcome pool of chemical healing. From time to time I change the water (shades of our changing systems!), thus making for the fish a vast discomfort. Besides, at any moment I could wash that whole cosmos down the drain, even though the fish may be spinning new psychological theories as the last word in truth, and building up national defenses "so that no enemy can defeat us." The kingdom has not yet come, but always it *is*, in encompassing and sovereign sway. Besides, it must come, and will come, because God is God.

III

We may now consider the bond between Christ and the kingdom, for there we shall find the central meaning of this prayer. His Incarnation and our human need both obliged Him to use our words. But He baptized every word in His purifying grace. The word kingdom received His shiningness and a new dimension. In Him it gathered heights and depths "as in heaven, so on earth."

He made the word an ethical universalism rather than a national favoritism. Already in the best Jewish insight it had that world-wide sweep and holy love; but what others had fitfully glimpsed, Jesus knew and ordained. Their foregleams were the "false dawns" that quicken hope after the long Arctic night; He was very sunrise. We are slow to learn this world-wide sway. Hitler imposed a "new order" on unwilling peoples; Stalin imagines himself the pioneer of a final revolution; and, because pride is a virus in the blood and not merely a localized sore, there are Americans who believe that our form of democracy is the last word and reluctantly feed lands, however hungry, which will not re-enthrone "free enterprise." The "kingdom" in Christ gathers in all mankind, beyond all ideologies, by the holy love of His cross. How sharply Jesus crossed the nationalism of His day! He dared to remind

His own townsfolk that God once sent a prophet to a Phoenician woman when no woman in Israel was ready to receive His word,[11] and another prophet to heal a Syrian leper rather than any leper in the "chosen" land.[12] Always the kingdom, interpreted by Christ, rebukes earthy motive and nationalistic narrowness.

Furthermore, the coming of the kingdom as Jesus construed it is an event, not a process.[13] This fact is hard for us to grasp, for we have been almost bewitched by the word evolution. But we are learning, even through our own science, that evolution is best understood as "emergence"; change comes by an unpredictable upsurge from some primal ground of life. This later knowledge is consonant with Jesus' word about the "kingdom." The parables in Matthew ring the changes on an *event*. The kingdom is like the sudden unearthing of buried treasure, or the appearance after long search of the priceless pearl, or the drawing of a dragnet full of fishes whereby the good fish can be chosen and the bad rejected. Even the parable of the seed [14] is in line with the proclamation of an event, for the emphasis there is not on growth, as our cult of evolution would like to assume, but on the helplessness of the farmer who can only "sleep, and rise night and day," on the sudden springing up of life, and on the farmer's wonderment because "he knoweth not how" the miracle is wrought. The kingdom is an event. The proper translation of "the kingdom of God is within you" [15] is therefore fairly certainly "the kingdom of God draws near" [16] in epochal event.

163

It follows that the kingdom is by God's gift, not by man's mind and hand. This truth is even harder for us to grasp. For proud man, especially since the Renaissance, has exploited the natural world as if he were the lord of creation. But man is creator only as he is first creature. He can fashion only as mind and hands are first given, and not even then except from materials placed in his hands. He is rightly awe-struck when a child is born; his act of inception is trivial compared with the marvel of new personality. He knows then that he cannot create life but only transmit it; even the kingdom of natural birth is birth "from above." Thus man can never be his own salvation; he can only receive God's salvation and proclaim the "good news." Because the kingdom is God's gift, Christ can describe it only in picture; our drab words are helpless to tell the heavenly grace. Thus the kingdom is celestial leaven hidden by God's hand in our earthiness, "treasure" of old and new drawn from a rich estate, a pearl of such surpassing worth that a man would wisely give everything he owns, even to his very life, to possess it.

Though the above-cited changes of meaning in the word "kingdom" are startling enough, the real revolution wrought by Jesus is still to be told: the kingdom came and comes in Him. He said, surely concerning Himself: "The kingdom of heaven is drawing near to you." [16] When His enemies accused Him of casting out devils by the help of the devil, He retorted that the devil was too wise thus to allow his house to be divided; and then he added, "But if it is by the Spirit of God that I cast out demons, then the kingdom of God has come upon you." [17] In Jesus the King has come by stealth of lowliness into our world. In the cross of Jesus He has joined battle in dread encounter with the defiance of the City of Mansoul and has conquered in love's seeming defeat. In the resurrection of Jesus and the gift of the Holy Spirit the light of the kingdom now streams in upon our darkened city, and who may hope to withstand its light? Our wars are not the thwarting of God's kingdom; they are the sign rather that men in the City of Mansoul fear the light, try to live in darkness, and so stumble over one another in violence. Jesus did not merely herald the kingdom, still less merely teach about it. It came and comes in Him. The early church was right in the evident stress laid on the story of the transfiguration: Christ was theophany, the breaking in of God upon our world, the promise of the "last days" when God will bring His will into plain sight in mingled judgment and mercy.

IV

Thus we reach some understanding of the prayer "Thy kingdom come." Our understanding grows each time we sincerely pray it, for thereby "light is sown for the righteous." [18] We confess that we know it must come, and that we have tried to resist its coming, and that we now surrender. Is there not a story of a cobbler at the siege of Paris who became so used to his dark cellar that he refused to come into the light? If we refuse, we die; and the kingdom becomes our judgment. "Thy kingdom come" means: "I walk into the light, as the banners of God's army move down the street. My darkened eyes are filled with pain, but I believe that soon the light will become joy. Nay, even now, through the pain, I see the glory of the King."

The prayer is likewise enlistment with the invasion of light. The praying man becomes a divinely "subversive agent," the spy of God in the City of Mansoul. He cannot bring the great day of the Lord, any more than he can create light. But he can reflect light. Outwardly he may seem no different from other men. He passes a friend in the street and says, "Hello, Jim"; he goes daily to the office and answers letters; he laughs and weeps as life brings happiness or sorrow; he dies at last as all men die. But he has a secret: he knows that the kingdom of light is just beyond the walls, and daily he receives its messages. So people find light in him and hardly guess its source. Then they say: "Perhaps there *is* something more than enlightened self-interest. Perhaps the clue *is* in Jesus." A worldly woman, having paid a social call on Alice Meynell, said afterward to a friend: "I feel somehow as if I must go to church and pray." [19]

But most of all the prayer is a *sursum corda:* "Lift up your heart!" Easily our eyes become filmed. The devil Screwtape, in *The Screwtape Letters,* [20] when he found a man under the sense of God and concerned about his soul, would suggest that it was "just about time he had some lunch." He would get him out-of-doors, for there he could easily persuade him that passing traffic and newspaper headlines are reality. As often as a man prays "Thy kingdom come," the line is open to the real World. He hears Morse signals from the encompassing Country. He has the secret; he knows that traffic and newspapers are only a shadow show, and that the banners that besiege the city walls are Reality. Already he has foretaste of heaven. Thus the prayer is pledge of the dawn. It is thanksgiving for life and light given in Christ. It is sure expectation. Once the prayer is sincerely prayed, the praying man has certitude, not in man's proud mind or grasping hands, still less in some new gadget, but in God; for God has come in Christ, and will come in His own good time to claim the city. The doctor prays the prayer and is no longer merely a doctor, whose patients all die at last; he is a witness for the kingdom. The teacher prays the prayer and is no longer merely a teacher, whose books yellow with age and whose words are lost in silence; he is a herald for Christ, and therefore the word of his life shall never die. "Thy kingdom come": the prayer is surrender, enlistment, and thanksgiving.

CHAPTER XII

The Will of God

"Thy will be done in earth, as it is in heaven."
Matthew 6:10

THE PSYCHOLOGISTS have the Rorschach test; they show a series of ink blots and ask the patient what each blot seems to picture. A fear psychosis, for instance, will reveal itself by imputing a threat to each innocent splotch. "The will of God" is an ink pattern on this page. What does it suggest? To some, a woman slowly dying of malignant disease: it is "the will of God." To others, a man refusing an attractive offer of work in the distant city because he must care for his ailing parents on the farm: he must resign himself to "the will of God." To others, a passenger plane struck by lightning, exploding, and plunging into the lake at midnight: this also is the inscrutable "will of God." To others, an inscription on a tombstone. Human nature seems prone to see a dark line in God's face. How far is this bent justified? It is so strong that it must have some basis. What is the will of God for men? Unless we know, at least in part, we can hardly pray this prayer with hope or wisdom.

I

Scholars are now generally agreed that Luke's account of the Lord's Prayer is earlier than Matthew's. This particular petition, as any reader can verify, does not occur in the Lukan version. Perhaps Matthew's rendering, written two generations after Jesus, reflects the needs and practice of the Syrian church; and perhaps its sevenfold form, while thoroughly true to Jesus, was designed for liturgical use at the celebration of the Eucharist. Scholars surmise therefore [1] that the third petition is a gloss on the earliest Prayer and has been added because of Gethsemane. For there Jesus besought God that the bitter "cup" of His foreshadowed death might "pass," but prayed nevertheless, "Thy will be done." [2] This surmise is strongly appealing, not only because it deals honestly with obvious differences in the manuscripts, but more because it derives this petition from the poignancy of Christ.

Such a theory, if sound, seems to support a somber view of "the will of God." Does it? Certainly this petition, by any theory, shows a clash between the human will and the Divine will. That the work of Jesus should end in failure, that the failure should spell apparent triumph for diabolic greed and pride, that evil should overwhelm Him in a wave so black that He must cry to His enemies, "This is your hour, and the power of darkness" [3]—this, surely, was not the will of God? But so it proved. There is always a clash between the human will and God's will. Rightly or wrongly, the human will seems a bright morning; rightly or wrongly, the Divine will often seems ominous night. The real line of conflict-choice is not between this nation's cause and that nation's, not between rival ideologies, not even between competing systems of ethics except on the surface; it is between the will of man and the will of God. The Fourth Gospel says that Jesus "went forth with his disciples over the brook Cedron, where there was a garden." [4] The garden was the Garden of Gethsemane. So the brook Cedron is the Great Divide of history. On that line all battles are fought.

II

Consider the human will. It is a real, if limited, freedom. Old Omar's word, that we are

> But helpless Pieces of the Game He plays
> Upon this Chequer-board of Nights and Days,[5]

has a certain appeal—perhaps because of the sad loveliness of the poetry, perhaps because it seems to rid us of the burden of responsibility, perhaps because it points to an indubitable Sovereignty—but it is still false to any man's experience. Almost every word in the dictionary refutes the poem. The word "coward," for instance, means that a man is free to be brave; and the sign "Keep Out" means that we are free to enter. Always the *arguments* are on the side of fixed fate; always our *instant assumptions* are on the side of free will, and we cannot help making the assumptions. We deduce by apparently unbreakable logic that we are bound, but we still assume that our brilliant argument is free. Not soon shall I forget the sight of a psychologist, famous for the doctrine that all our actions are but inevitable response to external stimuli, pleading with mothers to train their children in the theory. What use in pleading? Despite his doctrine, he had to assume that the mothers could choose to train their children in some other theory. It is foolish to argue against an inevitable assumption. Our will is a real, if limited, freedom.

Moreover, we pay honor, whether in folly or wisdom, to the thrust of the human will. Do we not say approvingly, "He is a man of indomitable will"? Concepts of right and wrong temper the approval, but do not break it; for graduating classes, which are not essentially different from other groups of people, when asked to state their choice of favorite "hero," have been known to choose Napoleon. Occidental man especially has been notable during the last century for laying strong hands on the planet, and on his weaker fellow men, to impose his purpose on the world. Witness our skyscrapers bastioned in rock, or the gash of a mine on the face of the landscape. This we approve; there is a poem lauding the fact that when men cut the Panama Canal from ocean to ocean, "the mountain stood aside." [6] The strong will does have merit, always provided it is directed to right ends. A weak will, whatever a man's other gifts, is timber without nails. But that "provided" with its "right ends" is a prodigious limitation. Perhaps it is the whole issue. Jesus spoke about power to move mountains, but He was intent on another goal.

For we could hardly claim that "the star of the un-conquered will" [7] (these phrases so dazzle us that we do not probe beneath the shining surface) has led us to a happy epoch. Certainly it has not brought us to the home of creative peace. How could it? If every member of a family is intent to exercise his own will, where is the guarantee that all will seek the family joy? For there is a cleft in man's will. He is tempted to will himself the center of his world, but he always knows through some sense of "pity" or "honor" that he is under constraint. That last word should be printed Constraint. When Shakespeare's apothecary sold poison suspecting that it was intended for murder, he excused himself: "My poverty, but not my will, consents." [8] But his will did consent, for he willed to be a party to murder rather than face poverty. He had chosen his own hankering or security, and rebelled against the Will that ordains that we live in "pity" and "honor." Do we ever really get away from that other Will? Why do we try? Is it because of the Devil's enticement at our weak point of creaturely anxiety, because of our fear of losing ourselves?

> For, though I knew His love Who followèd,
>   Yet I was sore adread
> Lest, having Him, I must have naught beside. [9]

Thus the Great Divide is the brook Cedron. We will either to stay in the Jerusalem of our self-centeredness, or to cross into the garden where we must pray "Thy will be done."

THE WILL OF GOD

III

Now consider God's will. We never escape it: a bird might as well try to escape the air. The stars obey the orbit of the Will, and perhaps that is why they "sang together" at the morning of the world. The flowers obey the Will; and therefore, so Jesus told us, they "grow" without any need of feverish "toil." All this we dismiss as "the pathetic fallacy," but perhaps it is our wilfulness that is pathetic, and perhaps flowers are a radiant sermon which we are too busy to heed. Dimly we know that beyond the mountains of mortality and our own steel fences there is a "heaven" where God's will is done. That the word "heaven" is in any dictionary is the sign royal on man's life. Are they angels who do the will of God "in heaven"? Shall we say of them that

> thousands at his bidding speed,
> And post o'er Land and Ocean without rest,[10]

and that sometimes they brush us with their wings, so gently that we do not speak of it lest we be branded fools? At any rate we guess, surely by some uncreated gleam, that there is a "heaven" where God's will is done; and it *is* heaven, not some dark line in God's face. Thus in one mood we imagine that God's will is enforced tragedy, and in another mood we conceive it as heaven.

Always we are in the will of God. We never escape. Man's will is free; but the freedom has limits, and the limits imply a wider realm by which man is still in bondage. We do not choose our parentage, and could not

173

if we would. We do not choose our color of skin or our aptitudes, and many people scowl at their meager equipment. We do not choose our place in history; and this generation, born under the sign of the atomic bomb, could fall prey to self-pity. We do not fully choose our course through life, for any man looks wonderingly at his own past and exclaims:

> There's a divinity that shapes our ends,
> Rough-hew them how we will.[11]

You whose eyes are on this page could not have governed the "chances" and changes that have brought you to your present post, and you did not will ten or twenty years ago that life should take precisely its present form. Another Will overrules our will, often to our "good fortune."

Yet there is a clash between our will and God's will. Perhaps we could not have known God except for the clash. For a child becomes aware of a world of other wills only when other children want the same toy at the same time. We older children become aware of God only when the world says No; for if the world always said Yes, we would assume that all events were by our magic. This is the dark line in God's face, or, at least, it is the line that seems dark to us. For life often goes against our desire, and we believe that our desires spell joy. We wish health, but soon or late meet illness. We covet life, but are obliged to die. Often the course we choose brings us to goals we do not choose; two world wars fought to bring peace are grim evidence. We willed the wars, or, rather, we willed

174

the economic and political prestige from which wars come; but we did not will the consequent chaos and fear. So we cannot escape the will of God. He counteracts and defeats many a purpose on which we have set our heart. It is not strange that this ink picture, the will of God, conjures up dark pictures such as that of a farmer gazing out on fields desolated by a dust storm. Seedtime and harvest are also God's will, but these coincide with our will and therefore in our pride we claim them; but dust storms are not our will, and therefore we ascribe them to God. As to the dust storms we are right; they are in some real measure God's will, directly or indirectly, and only a poor proximate thinking will try to ascribe them to some neutral "law of life." Nothing is neutral; if disasters come by law, there is still a Lawgiver. "The earth is the Lord's, and the fulness thereof." [12] But seedtime and harvest are also His. So His providence seems to man's eyes a succession of smiles and frowns.

IV

Our inquiry brings us to this paradox: our will is free, but only within the sovereignty of God's will. Why are we given any freedom? That we may voluntarily enlist under His will? We choose certain pleasures without let or hindrance; we choose certain other pleasures, and a Voice says, perhaps through the voice of the doctor, "If you walk that road, you will suffer pain leading to death." Shall we say that behind the "frowning providence" there is a "shining Face," and that our freedom is given that we may choose outright the often inscrutable will of God in the faith that He is good? So Tennyson taught, and he learned the truth through sorrow as he looked on Christ:

> Thou seemest human and divine,
> The highest, holiest manhood, thou.
> Our wills are ours, we know not how;
> Our wills are ours, to make them thine.[13]

Only two or three courses are open. We can rebel, but the rebellion will leave us stricken at last. Or we can endure stoically, which is what most people do, saying in dull resignation, "Well, that's life"; but the stoicism is a poor treadmill. Or in great venture of soul we may *choose* the will of God, as we say: "I see a smiling providence at times, and light has flashed on the world in Jesus Christ. Often life frowns, but I will believe that this also is for my good." Therefore the prayer: "Thy will be done." Jesus prayed it, and God has "given him a name which is above every name." [14]

The prayer means "Thy will be done" *to me* in alien providence. There *is* an accent of resignation, for, despite all our best endeavors, we must meet tragedy. Petitionary prayer is still valid. Indeed we cannot help pleading with God to fulfill our wish; that kind of prayer is as natural as breathing, and often God guides us through the granting of our wish. But petitionary prayer is both unreal and selfish unless "Thy will be done" is the final and saving chord in all its music. Indeed the praying man, as prayer purifies him, will find himself less and less disposed to bring his own wishes before God, and more and more eager that God's will be done. For the praying man learns to distrust his own wisdom. He notices that people rarely prosper in prosperity; they are more likely to "find themselves" in misfortune. So he does not quickly pray for comfort or uninterrupted good health; these threaten the soul more often than they save. He finds deep content in "Thy will be done." He lives in a creative acceptance of the Purpose who overrules all life. The dictum "His will is our peace" [15] is recognized as one of the sublimest truths outside the Bible. Do we remember its setting? In Dante's *Divina Commedia* it is the prayer of nuns who in their cloister and their own bodies have suffered spoliation by violent men, and are therefore placed in a lower level of heaven: "And his will is our peace." Thus they knew seventh heaven in their hearts.

The prayer also means "Thy will be done" *through me*. It is a yoke of service. Some disasters, or what we call disasters, cannot be avoided; but some can, and a true instinct bids us stop them. The description in law of public calamity as an "act of God" is sometimes just, for there are adversities beyond man's power to prevent; but sometimes the description is both a slander against God and a confession of our guilty laziness. The man who refuses to remove snow from his gas station because "God sends it, and why should I interfere?" is not talking sense; for God sent also the need to work, the power to work, the instinctive knowledge that a man must prevent adversity if he can, and the compassion that bids him labor for his neighbor's good. In 1792 William Carey preached a moving sermon on the text "Enlarge the place of thy tent," using it to plead with his congregation, "Expect great things from God, attempt great things from God." Thus was born the Baptist Missionary Society:[16] Carey himself went as missionary to India, and the congregation supported him, despite any who may have argued that it was God's will that the heathen should die in ignorance. But let warning be given: though the prayer means "Thy will be done" through me, there is still prime need to pray the prayer. For we easily substitute our will for God's will; and, though it is God's will that a swamp should be drained, it is not His will that the land thus reclaimed should be the site of a factory to manufacture burglar tools.

The prayer also means in great joy "Thy will be done" *for me and for all mankind*. For the will of God is not a dark line in God's face. It seems so only to our dim and shortened sight. Jesus said, "My meat is to do the will of him that sent me," [17] for the will of God is food and drink to our famished life. Sunrise is His will, and friends, and pardon for our sins, and the sure hope of life eternal. Only a misanthrope and ingrate mind could try to narrow the will of God to adversity. Gethsemane required Jesus to pray in a bleak midnight "Thy will be done," [18] but Gethsemane is now a shrine. We pretend that a few olive trees outside Jerusalem mark the site, and indeed that they were there when Jesus prayed, though the lapse of years and the siege of Jerusalem in

A.D. 70 plainly belie us. The beggars who infest the place ply their trade, not as pilgrims go to Gethsemane, but as they return; for beggars are shrewd to know when men's hearts are melted. Thus Gethsemane is a shrine and a fount of pity in our hardened world, because God's bleak midnight led to a brighter day. Jesus was wont to ask a man who came to Him for healing: "Wilt thou be made whole?" [19] The question meant, "Do you *will* to be made whole?" Behind the question was the reminder that wholeness would spell the end of self-pity and of many another selfishness. The will of God is always that we be made whole, through surgery perhaps, but with assurance of abounding health. So the prayer is a sound of trumpets now, on this side—the same trumpets that greeted Bunyan's Pilgrim "on the other side." [20]

V

There is a further paradox: only as a man surrenders his will to God is the man's will made strong. The Napoleons of "indomitable will" only provoke a clash of human wills that brings desolation, in which the indomitable will must surrender to a higher Will or die. But saints after the manner of Francis—"Praised be my Lord for our sister, the death of the body, from which no man escapeth. . . . Blessed are they who are found walking by Thy most holy will" [21]—know new power within their own will. So the envoys of the gospel, having surrendered their will to God, have shown a more indomitable will than any Napoleon. They have been

179

stronger to give than others to grab, and stronger to endure than others to strike. This is a paradox, after the truth of Paul's paradox: "Work out your own salvation with fear and trembling. For it is God which worketh in you both to will and to do of his good pleasure." [22] Thus the prayer "Thy will be done" is *the fulfillment* of the human will—"that ye may stand perfect and complete in all the will of God." [23]

CHAPTER XIII

God and Our Daily Bread

"Give us this day our daily bread."

Matthew 6:11

SURPRISINGLY THERE is a word in the Lord's Prayer which no one can translate. "Daily" is a guess, and not far from a blind guess. For the word *epiousion* occurs nowhere else in the New Testament, except in Luke's version of the Prayer, and nowhere in Greek non-Christian writings save for one papyrus. The latter is a leaf from a cook's household account, and the elusive word comes in an entry under the fifteenth day, perhaps in connection with a semimonthly reckoning.[1] This lone reference therefore seems to support such a translation as "daily" or "everyday." Scholars suggest various derivations for the word. The four that have most probability would result in the following: (a) necessary bread, (b) dependable bread, (c) daily bread, and (d) bread for the morrow. The reader may choose; he will have almost as much certainty as present scholarship. Perhaps the third and fourth have a slight edge in persuasiveness. If Matthew's version was used liturgically in evening worship,

181

"for the morrow" would have the force of "daily," and would not break Christ's injunction against anxiety for the morrow. He Himself would not have used a baffling word. Presumably the puzzle has come through the translation of His Aramaic into Greek.

Even the word "bread" has roused contention. Some commentators—Jerome, for instance, among the Church Fathers and Gerald Heard [2] among moderns—have argued that it means spiritual bread. Actually Jerome was not consistent, for he translated Matthew's version "supernatural bread," and Luke's version "daily bread." [3] Perhaps the inconsistency has merit, for "bread" in the whole range of Jesus' teaching meant both bread of earth and bread of heaven. Most scholars believe that "bread" in the Lord's Prayer means bread on our table. Why not? A saint must eat. Most people, who are not saints, must struggle for food. All prayer would die on our lips but for bread. Jesus made feeding the hungry a crux of judgment, the test that separates good men from bad men. [4] The Lord's Prayer is not a "heaven too high for our upreaching," [5] or remote from daily need. It sets our whole mundane life within the "Name" and the "Kingdom" and the "Will."

I

This fourth petition implies that every man is a pensioner of God. We are creatures. We live in a dependence which no human skill or striving can ever lift. This truth is not palatable to our modern pride, but it is still truth.

We speak of a man of "independent means," but he is not independent of the soil or the seasons or imminent death. We say of another man that he has "ample security," but angels must smile at our childishness; the man cannot eat dollar bills for breakfast, and could not eat at all except for the fruitfulness and faithfulness of nature, over which he can exercise only the tiniest control. The plain fact is that we live in a vast Givenness. We are hopeless debtors to the generosity of God, and we must needs pray that the Mercy may not fail.

Our lazy minds are content with surface readings. We see a tractor moving down the furrows and straightway exclaim: "Our labor of hand and mind wins for us our 'economy of abundance'!" But what good would the tractor be, or the man who drives it, if there were no life in the seed and no fertility in the soil? We can gather seed and sow seed, but we cannot create seed. It is true that there could be no harvest without man's labor, but it is doubly true that he could not labor without gifts in him and gifts in nature. In similar shallowness we observe certain regularities in our world, such as the uniform journeyings of sun and planet, and exclaim: "We live by nature's laws." We discover the laws, though even that small finding would have been beyond us if there had been no prior gift of law and mind, so we half believe that we ordained the laws. The very word "law" begs the question, for in our human affairs there could be no law without the sanction and fidelity of personal will. Then what of cosmic affairs? Certainly nature's laws are not blind; they show a marvelous co-ordination between the mysterious subtlety of nature and the greater subtlety of our life. Wise men renounce these surface readings. They go "back of" tractors and laws:

> Back of the loaf is the snowy flour,
> And back of the flour the mill,
> And back of the mill is the wheat and the shower,
> And the sun and the Father's will.[6]

Life is a table where we wait as children. We are dependent, even though we are allowed to help "our Father" with the chores. Day by day we must pray: "Our Father, give us this day our daily bread."

It follows, in prodigious consequence, that our material world is a sacrament. "Look for the stamp of the manufacturer," our advertising says, thus warning us against poorer goods. If only we did look for the stamp of the Manufacturer! To Him alone that word belongs: manufacture, *manu facere*, make by hand. For in His creation there is no dreary mass production by machine; everything wears the mark of loving handicraft. Fields and mountains speak of Him; they are sacramental, the outward and visible sign of an inward and invisible Spirit. This page before your eyes has His watermark on it. So has the eye that reads it. If we thought on the prayer as we pray it, the whole realm of our toil would be changed; or we would quit praying the prayer; or—is this the alternative we choose?—we would live in painful tension and in divided soul. At Iona, the bread for the Sacrament is a loaf baked in the kitchen of the brotherhood and carried down the aisle by the hands that baked it.[7] When this prayer is sincere, it requires of us that our toil must become such that we can carry it to the Holy Table.

II

The prayer "Give us our daily bread" is so rich in meaning that it is really a collection of prayers. This prayer is implied: Lord, that I may be faithful in my daily work! For God gives bread, not by lowering baskets of provisions from the sky, but through man's labor. The book of Genesis proposes that labor is a curse, a punishment on the race for the sin of Cain.[8] It becomes a curse if the mark of Cain is on it, if a man so labors that he hurts his brother man, or if the laborer is intent only on the pay check. But the carpenter shop at Nazareth was no curse, for surely He made houses and yokes for oxen and children's toys that were worthy in craftsmanship and serviceable in each day's life; and surely He gave stanchness and cheer through the labor. A man should do his share of the honorable work of our world. In a novel by Jozua M. W. Schwartz, Ursula hears that Otto van Helmont, son of the baron of the near-by castle, has broken the custom of his rank and is now earning his daily bread. "It seems so ridiculous, a van Helmont earning his living!" she exclaims.

Her father, the village pastor, replies: " 'Give us this day our daily bread.' That means: We would accept it, Lord, from no other hands but Thine."

She asks, "As manna?"

And he answers again, "No, child, as the harvest of toil." [9]

A man must not be a parasite on his fellow men, either as employer or employee. To indulge in sharp practice is to be a parasite. To charge "all the traffic will bear" is to be a parasite. To waste strength on work that adds nothing to the commonwealth is to be a parasite. "Give us this day our daily bread"—as the harvest of honest toil!

Another prayer is hidden in this fourth petition: Lord, that I may live in childlike trust! This prayer for bread is urgent, as if from a man hungry or not sure of his next meal. Perhaps Jesus had known hunger; his home was poor. Many of his compatriots lived close to the edge of subsistence, and all were burdened by Roman taxation. It is hard to face possible hunger; millions of men in our time have been ready to forgo political freedom rather than live in penury. Every one of us is tempted to say: "What if I should lose my job? What if long sickness should come?" As a matter of fact, the richest man is never far from starvation, for at any harvesttime the granaries of the world are almost empty. So "Give us this day our daily bread" is a prayer uttered in day-by-day trust. Anxiety easily besets us; but, far from helping, it poisons the mind and thus fetters our labor. We can either worry or trust. Jesus bade us trust. He lived in a faith that seems to us almost naïve: "Look at the birds . . . your heavenly Father feeds them." [10] Beyond doubt

He believed, and would have us believe, that God keeps the trusting man until his word is spoken and his work is done. James Smetham has described this childlike confidence:

It is not helpless submission to necessity. It is not the fulfilment of our roving desires. . . . One of its conditions is the perception of our proper place in the universe, and the belief that we have strictly a vocation. Another is that cheerful humility of spirit which honor upholds, and which makes no extravagant demands on the Universe or on Providence. Another is the alchymic eye to see much in little—the spirit which made the old woman say to Bishop Burnet, as she held up her crust, "All this and Christ." [11]

"No extravagant demands" is a phrase that points us to yet another prayer hidden in the fourth petition of the Lord's Prayer: Lord, that I may be content with a simple life! Bread is the request, not cake and comfort. In our time an "economy of abundance" is held before us as a political promise. Is it a promise or a threat? Manufacturers and their salesmen take for granted that there is "ceiling unlimited" for their wares. Is there, or does man always live within limits? The sharper question is this: Ought there to be no ceiling on material possessions? The answer to that second question is beyond doubt: a clutter of goods usurps the mind, arouses envy, and breeds pride. Emerson wrote: "My household suffers from too many servants. My cow milks me." [12] A man who thinks he owns "much goods" is actually owned by them. Of course the impoverished millions among mankind ought to have a reasonable security. That indeed is implied in

187

Christ's own prayer, for the word "bread" covers food, clothing, shelter, and every due material need. Of course there is enough and to spare for that brotherliness. Perhaps we should add that some men, such as doctors and judges and rulers, ought to be free from worldly anxiety, though such a plea could easily become a rationalization. But the fact remains that Christ believed in simplicity of living—"A man's life consisteth not in the abundance of the things which he possesseth" [13]—and that human experience, in the long history of pride and envy, has witnessed to His truth. A husband and wife were telling how the war had cut their living: they no longer had car, household help, or a Florida vacation. "If it were not for the war," they said, "we would be happier." "Bread" is the index of a simple life, and the prayer asks only for bread.

III

Now for the personal pronoun in the prayer: "us." Always it competes with the pronoun "I," and usually "I" wins. But the fourth petition is either a unison prayer, or the prayer of a man who knows that he must live within mankind's family bond. We should need no reminder. Mankind is an organism so sensitive that stocks rise or fall according to what is said in Ankara or Moscow, and men dear to us die in war in remote towns whose names were learned and forgotten in our school-day geographies. Isolationism is worse than political fallacy: it is religious blasphemy; for if there is one God, there is perforce only one family of mankind.

We can deny the fact of mankind's oneness, but the denial, like any other flouting of the human organism, brings sickness. Communism is a revolt of the impoverished masses. It thrives, not on its creed, but on human hunger. Poverty and hopelessness are always a hunting ground for the demagogue. There he finds ready prey. Thus demagoguery is the sickness which selfishness brings on the family. The basic question is not one of "free enterprise" versus "labor unionism," but the question of good manners; people seated at the family table ought to be willing to pass the bread. Better to do it gladly for Christ's sake than to do it by the compulsions of war and social revolt! George Washington Carver found a blue pigment in the clay of an Alabama hillside, after a group of businessmen had found nothing of particular value. They had been ready to sell the land for $7,000, but because of the discovery of a Negro scientist, they would not sell then for any figure short of a fortune. They offered him what they called "well-earned" riches, but he refused and would not even have his name advertised. He did try to patent his discovery, but the patent was broken.[14] So an improved blue came on the market, with a few men making the profit, though Tuskegee Institute and the Negroes of Alabama needed the money in almost a life-and-death need. Who had real right to the money? In what proportion? Negroes and white men alike are supported by a world-wide community of labor. As for the Negroes, they were originally brought as slaves from Africa. Who had larger right to the money? Perhaps we had better not press the question; it has very sharp points. Some men try to corner the bread at the table, taking more than they can eat; while other members of the family go hungry. The Red Cross is a happier instance. It recognizes that some people are in comfort, while others are being ridden down by the Four Horsemen—War, Pestilence, Famine, and Death. So the Red Cross speeds the passing of the bread at the family table, not as "charity" or a "dole," but in acknowledgment of family rights. A man does not give to the Red Cross; he puts the bread on the table where it belongs, instead of sneaking off with the whole loaf hidden under his coat.

"Our daily bread" is everybody's daily bread, the family bread. In a play concerning the great depression of the early thirties, a woman is shown watching the electric-sign announcements that run across the Times Building. The news was bad—the closing of banks and the threat of hunger. Suddenly she cried: "Our Father who art . . . in Heaven, Forgive us our daily bread." [15] Neither she nor the playwright made any mistake. The risen Jesus, so we are told in a gospel chapter edged with sunset light and promise of a fair morrow, overtook incognito two obscure disciples who were trudging home in sorrow for His death. They should have guessed the name of their Companion, for their hearts "burned" with hope as He walked and talked with them. Yet they were blind until they reached their home, until the moment when "He took the bread . . . and broke it." [16] Then they knew. Perhaps we shall never know Him, and shall still sorrow, until all bread is broken by Him and given to all. "Give *us* this day *our* daily bread."

IV

Nothing thus far written nullifies the cogency of the Jerome translation: *Panem nostrum supersubstantialem da nobis hodie*.[17] Perhaps "daily" has an eschatological stress; men then lived a day at a time in expectation of the imminent judgment at the "last days." In any event, Christ came because man "shall not" and cannot "live by bread alone." [18] This we all know; for when sorrow or grave anxiety comes, we push away the plate, saying "I do not feel like eating anything." Of the seven petitions in the Matthaean version of the Lord's Prayer only one concerns material bread. Even that petition does not concern "bread alone"; for prayers are offered, not to a celestial baker, but to the God and Father of our Lord Jesus Christ. God is our Father, and our main need is not for food, but for a homelike soul. Emerson has written: "Man does not live by bread alone, but by faith, by admiration, by sympathy" [19]—not a profound saying, unless we change it to "by faith in God, by fealty-admiration for Jesus Christ, and by sympathy born of God's love for us through Jesus." In the early church the fourth petition was sometimes phrased "Thy bread give unto us," [20] and there is an Irish manuscript of the eleventh century which reads, "Give us to-day for bread the Word of God from heaven." [21] Both prayers, for bread and for heavenly bread, find warrant in the life and light of Jesus. So why should not both be implied in this petition?

It could be argued that our generation has tried to live by "bread alone," and therefore is in danger of losing even earthy good by atomic desolation. If conscience is only custom, pity only a trick of the nerves, and Jesus only a sentimentalism, nothing better than chaos is in store; for in such a world, without landmarks for the soul, every man is an enemy. How we need living Bread: "This is my body, which is broken for you"! [22] Of this Bread also the prayer is for "*daily*" Providence. No man can live on the religion of his fathers. The children of Israel found that the manna given in the desert did not keep; it had to be gathered each day. The vision of our youth or some vow made in sickness last year is not enough food for today; the prayer must be each day's entreaty.

Jesus did not mock men; He would not have taught a futile prayer. His "when ye pray, say" is the promise of prayer's power, or, rather, of the power of God given to hands opened by prayer to receive His gifts. The fact that we do not always "feel" the answer to prayer should not discourage us. A sailor measures his progress by the stars, not by the thermometer in the cabin. We need not constantly take our spiritual temperature. The prayer for bread of body is answered: God keeps a man on earth until the man's vocation is fulfilled, for, even if the man starve by the callousness of his neighbors, God can turn that surrender to the kingdom's coming—as He turned a vaster Calvary. The prayer for bread of soul is answered, "more and more unto the perfect day." [23]

CHAPTER XIV

The Prayer for Pardon

"And forgive us our debts, as we forgive our debtors."
Matthew 6:12

SOME PROTESTANT churches use the word "debts," others say "trespasses." In the former group, for instance, are most of the churches of the Reformed faith; in the latter, for instance, the Protestant Episcopal Church. The layman is baffled. When he worships in a strange church, he comes to an awkward pause in the greatest of all prayers, because he does not know which word the minister will use. He wonders why the churches do not "get together"; and, if he remembers that our New Testament is a translation from the Greek, he finds it hard to believe that one Greek word can have two somewhat divergent meanings.

Perhaps the break cannot be justified, but it can be explained. The word in the Matthew manuscript is *opheilēmata,* which means debts. Two verses later, in the phrase translated in the King James Version "trespasses," the word is *paraptōmata,* which in its root means missing the mark. In the Luke manuscript the word is *hamartias,*

193

which means sins and is so translated in the King James Version. Tyndale translated Matthew's first word "trespasses." [1] The Book of Common Prayer followed him; hence the wide use of that word. The King James Bible rendered Matthew's first word "debts," and the second word "trespasses"; hence the wide use of "debts." Should the churches "get together"? Of course, on any one of the three English words, for they all have the same central meaning. It is a misfortune that English-speaking followers of Christ are not fully united in the Prayer He taught.

I

By any translation the Prayer takes for granted our failure. The transgression is not argued but simply assumed. Is there room for argument, except among the calloused, the fractious, or the merely dilettante in mind? Actually the sense of guilt is a mark of nobleness, for only men and angels can fall. If we deny guilt, we deny virtue. For consider: if Hitlerism is not dastardly, there are no standards; and therefore a Gandhi had no love for his fellow men. If we cancel the word sin, bravery and cowardice alike are but a sound of words "signifying nothing," and our whole life but a shadow show. "Forgive us our debts" is condemnation indeed, but it is much more: it is the assurance that man is made to live in response to God.

By any word—debts, missing the mark, trespasses—our failure is written large in black letters. As for debts,

194

have we paid all we owe to ourselves and our neighbors—
and to God? One fact alone, our shabby forgetfulness
of a hundred martyrs who have died for our liberty, is
enough to declare us bankrupt. As for missing the mark,
a baseball manager recently resigned with the comment,
"I have not done what I set out to do," [2] thus speaking
for every man; and, if we miss our own mark, how much
more the "mark . . . of the high calling of God in Christ
Jesus." [3] As for transgressions, have we not trespassed,
like any poacher or fence breaker, on holy ground? The
Church has blundered, not in condemning sin, but in
failure to show that the sense of sin is the concave of the
human lens, and that there is always a convex of yearned-
for saintliness. The saints have been more acutely aware
of sin precisely because they are saints; their convex,
more rounded out towards God, has implied a deeper
concave. Thus Paul's "sinners; of whom I am chief" [4]
is thoroughly sincere: it is the concave of his convex reflection of God's light. The sense of sin can become mor-
bid, as psychology has shown; but by the same token it
can become casual—a worse fate, for as we lose awareness that we are earthy, we thus lose touch with heaven.

There are social sins, so black that we do in groups
what we would not dream of doing in lonely conscience;
lynching or obliteration bombing are instances of a group
deviltry whose name is Legion. Few individuals would
hand a club to a bully to beat a helpless victim, but
civilized nations sold armaments to Japan when Japan
wantonly invaded China. Who would see a man starve

to death on his doorstep? But mass famine in India arouses in America or Europe no unbearable pain.

Our tendency nowadays is to condone the individual; he may be the victim of his home situation or social environment. But that judgment, in frequent instances true, lays the heavier blame on the family and the community. And therefore on individuals, for the fact of individuality can hardly be denied. Our separateness in body is but the sign of a hidden separateness so invincible that nobody really knows his neighbor. Thus the "failure of the home" does not cancel single responsibility; it saddles it on this father and this mother and this brother. Advertising cheapness is due at long last to this publicity man, that merchant, and the other editor or radio announcer. Our tendency to blame the group in the hope that thus guilt will run out, spread thin, and disappear is a vain refuge; a German pastor rightly said of the Hitler regime, when he could easily have laid a vague charge against "the government," "I should have spoken, and I was silent." [5]

Thus the "our" in "our debts" is both editorially and literally true, and the prayer is rightly addressed to God because our sins are against Him. The phrases "he is hurting himself" and "his conduct is antisocial" are both just, but they are short-circuited: behind a man and his neighbor is God. Even an atheist, who shies at the word God, would have to use some such word as Process or Life when describing transgression. Our deepest sin is sin against Life. The child was deeply wise who, when his mother forgave him a falsehood and told him that "everything is all right now," answered, "But I still told a lie." That child's mind is more profound than the kind of thinking that rests in such terms as "antisocial." We are in debt. We have not paid what we owe. Loans on life are at interest, so the debt mounts. Thus we are "drowned debtors"; we can only pray: "Forgive us our debts."

II

We ourselves can never extricate ourselves from debt. For life is an inexorable movement in a one-way direction: we cannot go back or stay life's course. If a man were one hundred per cent honest today, as he never is, he has not canceled yesterday's dishonor; and that dishonor meanwhile has spread through the common life like ink in water. There is truth in our blame of the past —Adam blamed Eve, and Eve blamed the serpent, as the psychologist today blames a father's coercions or a mother's indulgences. But so long as we are responsible at all, some measure of guilt belongs to every man. The past is past, but it is present in the memory; and no man can cleanse his memory. The Negro spiritual "Were you there when they crucified my Lord?" [6] is an appeal to remorseful memory. The sharpness of the question implies that no man can cleanse his memory; he may drug it, but he cannot cleanse it. Perhaps it also implies that a crucified Lord can do for the memory what a man can never do. But, as to that, let us take one step at a time. No man can recover the past; no man can cleanse his

197

memory; no man can act for violated Life. Here only God can help us, and our only weapon is a prayer: "Forgive us our debts."

We have suggested that in the original prayer there may have been only three petitions: "Thy kingdom come, give us our daily bread, and forgive our sins." This is no more than a surmise, though there is some evidence to support it. We do not know, for we have no original autograph. But supposing the suggestion to be correct, it is not strange that the prayer for bread should be followed by the prayer for pardon. The one is bread for the body; the other is bread for the soul—the very renewal of our inner life. The one is as much beyond the power of man alone as the other; we can no more contrive new motives than we can contrive sun and rain. We are as hungry for one as for the other; famine of body is perhaps easier to bear than famine of soul, and every man cries in his solitude

> Ah for a man to arise in me,
> That the man I am may cease to be! [7]

No Buddhist doctrine of the transmigration of souls, whereby man works out his own salvation, can content us; for we dimly know that our very will is weak and that to ask us to save ourselves is like inviting a drowning man to swim. Incidentally this one instance of difference between Buddhist and Christian faith disproves the shallow doctrine that "all religions are true." How can they all be true if they stand in contradiction?

A wound heals by nature's ministries, the doctor being only nature's skillful aide. The cure in new tissue comes from an encompassing "beyond" that is yet near. How is heart or conscience healed? Despite Macbeth's doctor, no man can "minister to himself" [8] in this crisis. Is there a gracious Beyond that is yet Nearness? Gerald Heard has asked the real question: "How do you manufacture ... white corpuscles?" [9] Forgiveness is not mere acquittal; it is a re-creation. It is a new alliance with God and consequently a new alliance with man; and therefore only God can work the change. Not easily, for all creation is pain, and re-creation is double pain. Perhaps God must say what we say: "I could more easily begin again than change it."

Not easily, for God is righteousness in love, and all contact with sin is pain for Him. Pierre Corneille, in his tragedy *Cinna,* makes Auguste say: *"Qui pardonne aisément invite à l'offenser"*—He who pardons easily invites offense.[10] Most people today would agree, but the whole sentiment is still a mistake. The catch is in "easily." There is no easy pardon. He who pardons easily does not pardon at all. Pardon is not mere forgetting; a noble mother does not merely forget the shame of her wayward son. She remembers it, yet forgives, in the daily travail of a holy soul. The forgiveness is not easy even for the son. He can receive it only as a man receives light, and light is painful for long-closed eyes. Think of Jesus washing the feet of Judas just prior to the betrayal! Already

Jesus forgave him—"while we were yet sinners"! [11] But Jesus grieved, suffered, and died—and thus forgave.

III

"Think of Christ": He alone could teach the prayer in its fullness. For He alone shares every man's life; He wins each eye, like the central sun. He alone shares God's life, for He alone shows no disfigurement of failure. So we see in His grief on Calvary the holy travail of God's love. Somewhere I have read of a transfusion of blood in which a father's vein was drawn from his body and stitched into a vein of his ailing child, that the flow of his blood would be warm and without clot. He was asked if the affair hurt and answered: "It hurts like hell, but that does not matter." No parable can more than hint the ways of God. But is not Christ a living vein drawn from the very life of God, so that *through* Him, stitched into our very humanity, new life flows into our world? Thus the redemption of history—from beyond history! Thus the redemption of every man's life, so that you and I can each say, "[He] loved me, and gave himself for me"! [12]

The gift is free, even as it is beyond price. Each day a man must pray "Give us bread," and bread is given; each day he must pray "Forgive our debts," and the new indebtedness is canceled in new life. That is why our guilty sickness does not utterly destroy us; God gives white corpuscles. The gift cannot be purchased by any imagined "goodness" or "penance": "For by grace are ye saved through faith; and that not of yourselves: it is the gift of God." [13] It is true that the penalty of sin remains, but the penalty is not now penalty but discipline and the reminder of God's goodness. The marks of the far country were doubtless on the prodigal as long as he lived, but they were not a brand such as governments were wont to burn on the flesh of a convict; they were now a yoke in which the prodigal plowed mightily in God's field—the means, for instance, whereby the once-prodigal dealt patiently and lovingly with the failures of his neighbors. The history of the soul knows, far better than the skill of modern industry, that "waste products" can prove to have greater value than the main output.

Then it would pay a man to sin? To that question we can only answer in instant horror, as Paul answered, "God forbid!" [14] Such deviltry would turn light into darkness and remove all chance of pardon. A man trying to play the part of sun and rain would be a megalomaniac in very truth; and a double mania of guilt would rest on a man trying to play the part of Calvary and a pardoning Throne. We are creatures; we can only pray for bread, not contrive it. We are creatures; we can only pray for pardon, not devise it. If we try to play sleight with God's hand, we are thrust into outer darkness, because we have chosen to call darkness our light. Only one thing can we do, and it is enough: we can pray "Forgive us our debts."

IV

Then what of the ominous addendum, "as we forgive our debtors"? The exact translation of the Matthaean version is "as we also have forgiven our debtors." Luke's version says, in exact rendering, "for we ourselves forgive everyone who is indebted to us." [15] The Old Syriac manuscript reads, in both Matthew and Luke, "Remit to us, and we also will remit." [16] Thus in the various manuscripts we can find this proviso in all three tenses. But, as for the past, *have* we forgiven? As for the present, *do* we forgive? As for the future, is there any sure promise that we *will* forgive? The proviso seems to kill all hope of answer to the main prayer.

But, for our reassurance, the qualifying phrase is not a *quid pro quo;* it does not mean that God forgives only in equal measure as we are willing to forgive. Such an "equal" would condemn our world. God is "Our Father," not the keeper of celestial ledgers. Dr. William Manson's comment gives light: "The clause . . . states not the ground on which God bestows forgiveness but the ground on which man can receive it." [17] God's pardon predisposes us to pardon those who have hurt us, as we hope they will pardon us for hurt we have done. If we act on the predisposition—and indeed on the power which only God's pardon can give us—His pardon continues to flow; but if we, pardoned of God, do not try to pardon our brother, we block the channel by which God's pardon finds us. All God's gifts must be shared or they are stopped, not least God's gift of forgiveness. This truth is so crucial that only for this petition of the Prayer did Jesus give an explanation.

The proviso ought to be clear: a child who says to the

brother with whom he is quarreling, "I'll never forgive you," is in no mood to be forgiven by his father. He has no wish then to be forgiven. It is not in all his thoughts. He is intent only on his brother's wrong and his own hurt pride. How, in that bitterness, can his father even approach him? When Queen Caroline's death was announced, Lord Chesterfield is supposed to have said, "And unforgiving, unforgiven dies." [18] The two words are twin, just as forgiving and forgiven are twin. This truth is reiterated in the teaching of Jesus. He said that a man bringing a gift to the altar, yet hugging a grudge against his neighbor, had better go and be reconciled; God cannot use a poisoned gift. Jesus told a story, furthermore, of an overseer who was forgiven a vast indebtedness by his master, but promptly threw into prison a man who owed him (the overseer) a trifling sum. "And his lord was wroth, and delivered him to the tormentors." [19] Of course—the mind that harbors an enmity is always in torment.

We do not fulfill the proviso, so there is little of the grace of God in us. Sometimes we "forgive" so casually as to show that we are casual about any right or wrong; but real forgiveness, far from being morally indifferent, is aflame with truth and must redeem a lie. Sometimes we "forgive" while insisting that we shall never "forget"— a pardon that is not pardon but only a temporary concession from wounded pride. God's pardon is nothing less than the gift of new life in our guilty sickness, by travail of love; and man's forgiveness is nothing less than the sharing of that love, in patient pain of persistent good will. There is little such forgiveness in our world. Law courts prove the lack: people "get even" rather than resolve under God to bring new life to the wrongdoer. The history of nations proves it: Germany's second attack on Europe, though black-stained with guilt, was not unrelated to the blockade during the first World War, a blockade that was kept for eighteen months after armistice. Pardon for Germany does not mean the equating of right and wrong, as though Hitler's deviltry were to be treated no differently from Norway's resistance to him; it means precisely the opposite—a recognition of the wrong, yet a dealing with it in persistent, realistic, long-suffering good will. Because of the lack of that pardon in our world, hate breeds hate, and war breeds war, in endless cycle. That cycle only pardon can cut—God's pardon empowering man's pardon.

V

Our safeguard is to keep on praying the prayer: "Forgive us our debts." Then as we know the measure of our indebtedness and the vaster measure of renewing grace, bitterness will yield place in us, and we shall be ready to add "as we forgive our debtors." For "to err is human, to forgive divine" [20]—divine in a deeper sense than Alexander Pope intended, divine in the sense that only God can give it. Only God can forgive sins, and He only as by pain of His love He gives us His life. Only God can quicken in us the forgiving spirit.

In castles of the old world, visitors are shown hidden doors leading to secret passages and are told: "This is how help came when the castle was held in unbreakable siege." Mankind is a prisoner to a helpless will and a mind of enmity, but there is a secret way. Any man still has contact with a vast Country beyond his beleaguered self, for he can pray: "Forgive us our debts, as we forgive our debtors." Then, as a forgiven man, he can say to his brother, "I forgive you, as I trust you to forgive me." Thus the siege is lifted. "Be ye kind one to another, tenderhearted, forgiving one another, even as God for Christ's sake hath forgiven you." [21]

CHAPTER XV

The Prayer for Deliverance from Evil

"And lead us not into temptation, but deliver us from evil."   Matthew 6:13

THIS PRAYER AT first sight is hard to understand. There is some trouble in the word "lead," which when accurately translated is "bring," and much more trouble in the word "temptation." If the latter means test or trial (and that is what it did mainly mean when the King James Version was made), is not testing good for us? And should we ask God not to lead us into it, but to bless our cowardice? If, on the other hand, "temptation" means seduction to evil, does God seduce? And must we beseech Him not to act like a devil? Some commentators have tried to limit the word to its meaning of trial, and have sought warrant through the Aramaic in which Jesus spoke. So they propose such a translation as Dr. Charles Cutler Torrey's: "And let us not succumb at the time of trial." [1] That, if true, would safeguard both realism and courage; but we cannot be very sure about the original Aramaic. Other commentators find escape through the verb "lead": they have argued that the petition means

"Have us not brought into temptation," [2] the onus for seduction thus being laid on man and the devil rather than on God, He being asked to play His proper role of Deliverer.

What *does* the prayer mean? Only the first phrase is found in early Lukan manuscripts. Has Matthew amplified the original prayer, which (perhaps) had only three or four petitions, into a sevenfold version for liturgical use? We have noted that "Thy will be done" was added, though in strict accord with Jesus' teaching. Seven was then a holy number. "Lead us not into temptation" would, by this theory, be the sixth petition, and "Deliver us from evil" would be the seventh; and the two would thus demand separate treatment, except for the "but" that joins them. The "but" seems to show that the two prayers are concerned with one issue—deliverance from evil. Most scholars agree that "temptation" in the original must have had that coloring. Such indeed seems to have been the assumption of the early church, for a controversy then raged about the origin of evil: *can* God seduce? The echoes of that strife are seen in the Epistle of James: "Let no man say when he is tempted, I am tempted of God." [3] Was the strife incited by pagan gibes and Christian bafflement at "Bring us not into temptation"? So Dr. William Manson suggests, not without persuasiveness. [4] We shall not evade the issue. Meanwhile let us notice this intriguing item: Matthew's liturgical version drew on the Gethsemane scene for "Thy will be done"; perhaps the suggestion came from this reminder of the garden, for did not Jesus there warn His disciples: "Watch and pray, that ye enter not into temptation"? [5]

I

The Greek word *peirasmon* does include the idea of test or trial. Every man needs test. This the petition seems tacitly to admit, for what would be the use of asking deliverance from evil if the struggle were unlikely or altogether alien from worthy conduct? A man who tries to avoid encounter with the world is a child rather than a man. Psychology knows him and his "arrested development." He is tied to his mother's apron strings. He covers his cowerings with the excuse that he is "needed at home." He is no joy to himself; his rationalizations, however clever, do not hide from him the fact that he has run away from life. Likewise he is no joy or help to his neighbors; he is a weak link in the communal chain. During World War II a few freighters, hurriedly built to maintain a supply line in a time of submarine threat, split amidships in heavy seas. The defect was in the welding or the over-all construction. A ship must be able to ride a storm, but there is no other way than storm to test the workmanship. When a man is applying for a job, one question almost sure to be asked of him is, "What's your experience?" which is but another way of inquiring if he has been tested. Testing, other things being equal, is a good.

Perhaps every man needs also seduction. If the reader bridles at that word, he must still admit that every man needs to be confronted with alternative good and evil, so that he can make his choice (not without urgency and prayer) , and thus choose good as a bannered cause. Automatic goodness is a contradiction in terms. For "nothing . . . can . . . be regarded as good . . . except the good will." [6] But such an admission involves enticement, despite our bridling, and recognizes its place in the growth of souls. Jesus was "tempted of the devil" [7] according to one Gospel, and according to another was "led by the Spirit into the wilderness, being . . . tempted of the devil"; [8] and there is not necessarily any contradiction in the two accounts. Thomas Henry Huxley declared that he would gladly be turned into a clock if "some great Power" would agree thus to make him "always do . . . right"; for, he added, "the only freedom I care about is the freedom to do right." [9] But, of course, a clock is not free. There is no merit in a clock, despite our appraisals of "a good clock" or "a poor clock that does not keep time," for a clock ticks with an automatic tick; but there is merit in a clockmaker, for he is free to make a good clock or a poor clock. If a man is tempted, he has chance to choose and thereby become a worthier man. Temptation is thus a fork in the road, a way up or a way down; and, if God is man's Unseen Ally, temptation can be a blessing.

It is thus clear that both test and enticement may come in original good intent from God. No man lives without trial, however he may seek escape; he is "born unto trouble, as the sparks fly upward," [10] though not without many a concordant joy. He must meet sickness and death. He must meet disappointment and the "blank misgivings of a creature." [11] Not often does a man know

> That blessed mood,
> In which the burthen of the mystery,
> In which the heavy and the weary weight
> Of all this unintelligible world,
> Is lightened.[12]

Likewise a man must meet enticement to evil. He may run to some lonely desert to avoid the conflict, but to no avail; for there he will find, like Anthony, that no desert can shut out devilish imaginings. That saint and his fellow hermits in the Sahara "battled with the most subtle temptations the devil could devise." [13] Indeed trials and temptations are never separate; life itself gives both meanings to the prayer. The Christian church where Matthew wrote—probably at the turn of the first century, perhaps in Syria—had to meet the test of persecution, but the test itself was the result of evil: namely, the coercive conservatisms of the synagogue and the brute pride of the Roman Empire. By whatever medium trials and temptations reach us—whether through men, or through some licensed devil, or through some fallen angel become a Prince of Wickedness, or through the evil inclinations of our own hearts, or by a conspiracy of wrong outside us and wrong within us—every man is both tried and enticed. This double stamp is indelible on man's life. So, in its origin or course, it must come by the consent of God. Plainly a man arrives at manhood by being tried and enticed.

II

So we declare and rightly believe. And that's the devil of it! For how confident we are, how incredibly sure of ourselves! We dramatize temptation in our secret thoughts, thus gathering gasoline for the devil's spark. We eagerly read books and see plays that depict wickedness—sometimes the portrayal is with so comely a disguise that fallen angels chuckle and leave their work to men. We even go across lots to seek enticement, playing our own providence, as if life of itself would not bring enough temptation. We deliberately sin "for the sake of experience," an excuse which is either a lie, or the conceited bravado by which a "human fly" crawls up the front of a skyscraper, or the senselessness that looks down a snake's throat in quest of information. If anybody warns us, he is an "old fogey." Was Jesus an "old fogey"? Even our brash modernisms would shrink from that slur; *He* warned us, in tones that have the accent of life-or-death. We claim that "to the pure all things are pure," [14] forgetting that the man who wrote the words was first sealed to Christ and knew that he could not live apart from Christ. To confess that trial and enticement have their place in the growth of souls gives us no permit to play the part of deity, or to experiment with evil, still less to make a snake pit and live in it.

What *is* evil? No negative term is enough for description; and if it were, it could not rid evil of its sting. Evil is not the greenness of the young tree; and if it were, a tree can by arrested development give only leaves. Evil is not the adolescence of the soul; and if it were, a man can be locked in adolescence and thus become a deformity. Evil is not "naught, . . . silence implying sound" [15] (as Browning was quick to tell us in many a poem, such as "Gold Hair") ; and if it were, silence can deal death to a man hungry for a Voice. Evil is not a "neurosis"; and if it were, a neurosis is by nature a bane and can become a cancer in the mind. Evil is not the counter stream against which we flex our swimming muscles; and if it were, the stream will sweep us to destruction if we lack strength. This prayer "Bring us not into temptation" is not logical? Perhaps prayers are not supposed to be logical; a swimmer unequal to the stream of life forgets logic and cries aloud. because he must: "Deliver me from evil."

Negative terms are not enough to portray evil. The origin of wickedness is an unplumbed mystery. No book, much less this book, can sound that dark depth. But there are facts to which any man can testify. Evil comes as if it were another voice, not simply as the echo of our own thoughts. A man may be walking along Fifth Avenue intent only on the sights—nay, he may even be uplifted in mind as he thinks on the kindness of a friend—when suddenly, as if some demon had fallen through air to whisper in his ear, a base treachery waylays him. The insinuating voice says not, "Brother, can you spare a dime?" but "Brother, can you spare your soul?" Jesus was tempted at the very point of nobleness: "If you *are* the Son of God . . ." [16] Is it strange, since evil has this objective character

212

of a sharply other voice, that men have framed doctrines of a "personal devil"? Experience is on their side.

Moreover, evil is organized in hierarchies of evil. Who does the organizing? A popular love song tells how love begins:

> You may see a stranger
> Across a crowded room.[17]

Unhappily that is also how wickedness spreads. The crook finds the crook, as if some unseen devil were drawing them together; and they form a fellowship of crooks—the narcotic ring, the political spoils system, Hitler's "new order." In a lunatic asylum the doctors are reasonably safe from violence; for a lunatic is an egotist turned sick in mind, and therefore lunatics do not have sense enough to join forces. The misadventures occur singly and can be handled. But devilishness is not lunatic; it is devilish in the skill and power of its organization. A crook in his single unruliness can be controlled, but a racket may victimize a nation or a world. Who does the organizing? Paul and his generation believed in an invisible kingdom of devils poised in the air between heaven and earth, ruled over by the prince of devils. He was far truer to any man's experience than shallow doctrines of evolution. His words have realism: "For we are not contending against flesh and blood, but against the principalities, against the powers, against the world rulers of this present darkness, against the spiritual hosts of wickedness in the heavenly places." [18]

213

Other signs might be noted of the hard-to-deny personalism of evil, as, for instance, evil's skill in disguise. Milton pictures the devil taking the form of an old rustic when he tried to trip Jesus. He seemed altogether innocent in nature and in purpose:

> Following, as seemed, the quest of some stray ewe,
> Or Wither'd sticks to gather, which might serve
> Against a winter's day, when winds blow keen.[19]

Surely such a man would appeal to the pity of Christ! Could any impersonal evil or immaturity be so apt and shrewd in design? Yet evil takes also an impalpable and almost abstract form, as for Pilgrim on the Enchanted Ground; for there Satan was not an Apollyon with darts or a Giant Despair with dungeoned castle, but only heaviness of eye and dullness of spirit.[20] Not strangely the New Testament sometimes speaks of "the evil," and sometimes of "the evil one." All we know is that evil takes now the nature of a mood or spirit, and now a form so sharply personal that we must postulate a "father of lies." But we can be sure, if we have any wisdom, that evil by any name is intent to slay us. Our age has evidence enough: we have seen evil, organized in demonic empire, calling falsehood by names of truth, delighting in wanton chaos and nothingness, until the whole planet is now under threat of atomic desolation. This is "the evil" with which we take chances, as we spin pleasant theories about "the ascent of man"!

III

If our own heart were sound, we might risk even a devil's contagion without any large dismay. But there is treachery within, inviting the outer foe:

> I said to Heart, "How goes it?" Heart replied:
> "Right as a Ribstone Pippin!" But it lied.[21]

Our educational theories assume, with almost incredible shallowness, that man is a reasonable creature who, when his reason is trained, can be trusted to act with all reasonableness. Freud punctured that pretense, and modern Germany is his witness. He taught, or rather underscored, what the Bible had already taught, that there is a subliminal irrationalism in man which may at any time erupt. The Bible language is simpler: "The heart is deceitful above all things, and desperately wicked: who can know it?" [22] Our education has no defense against that irrationalism, as educated Germany again proved, except by faith in a structure of Grace over against the "vasty deep" of the "unconscious." The man who says that "there will always be wars" is right if we have no resource beyond ourselves; for, as Jesus plainly told us, "out of the heart proceed . . . murders, . . . fornications, thefts, false witness, blasphemies." [23] The only ground for optimism is in the faith that man's nature is a paradox of devil-angel, and that from Beyond comes power to break the hyphen, destroy the devil, and enthrone the angel.

The weakness in man gives evil enticement its chance, as Achilles' heel invited Paris' arrow.[24] How temptation is matched to our years, as at adolescence or in "the foolish forties"! How diabolically it meets our occupation, so that a broker is enticed to become rich and a preacher to become self-righteous! How cleverly it is camouflaged: C. S. Lewis rightly contends that the word "puritanism" has been of late the best word in the devil's vocabulary.[25] How suddenly it besets us, like a thunderstorm, so that our hates are spoken as soon as thought! How stealthily it creeps on us, like numb death on a man who sleeps in snow! At the onset of this century we were quite sure that we had war chained like a circus bear. We could fill our house with furniture and gadgets, and live in peace, and perhaps even conquer death. Then suddenly the tame bear, another disguise of the devil, was upon us. Perversity outside us and within has cankered over twenty civilizations. It has turned our technology into destruction and made democracies more warlike than kingdoms. Such facts are not an argument for kingdoms as against democracies, but simply a tracing of the fact that evil can turn the better into the worse and overwhelm supposedly good men by "the power of darkness." [26] Perhaps the sixth and seventh petitions of the Lord's Prayer are not good dialectic. But they give realistic voice to our weakness: "Bring us not into temptation." They know the power of the foe and the helplessness of human resource: "Deliver us from evil." So they are true theology and a final dialectic of our earthly life.

IV

If there is a devil in our world, and within us a treachery that is a "fifth column" for the devil, it follows that unaided man is helpless. To ask him to gird up his will to live nobly is like asking a man with a broken arm to strike a mighty blow, for the weakness in us is at the very point of the will. The growth of our body, airplanes being longer legs and machines being multiplied fingers, has hidden from us the infirmity of our will. But C. E. M. Joad is the forerunner of moderns who begin to understand. He had told us in his *God and Evil* [27] that he became convinced, though he had long been an agnostic in religion, that the wickedness of a concentration camp is wicked, not simply the result of personal or social frustrations; and that once he was driven to that conclusion, he could not escape the further truth that man is helpless, inwardly cleft and outwardly threatened, unless God comes to his help. The reality of evil in our world, and the hopelessness of that fact if man stands alone, drove him back to a faith in the reality of God. Behind the urgency of Jesus and His reiterated "watch and pray" is precisely that fact: man is helpless without God. If we had clear eyes, we would see that such a helplessness is at root not weakness but our best power, the force that carries us to our nature's true fulfillment: "Thou madest us for Thyself." [28]

The myths foreshadow not only this need of man for heaven's help, but also heaven's readiness to stoop to earth. Thus fire, without which earth is cold and dark, is a celestial gift brought by Prometheus[29] at bitter cost. The story is a clear hint of Him who came with the diviner flame: "I am come to send fire on the earth; . . . and how am I straitened till it be accomplished!" [30] The myth of

217

St. George and the Dragon underscores even more sharply man's helplessness and heaven's help. The dragon is the power of evil. He devoured first the fields, then two sheep each day, then two children, and finally demanded the king's only daughter—a progression that vividly depicts the fate of those who parley with evil and feed it. Then came the hero-soul from beyond those bounds. Rightly he made the sign of the cross and named the Name of Christ. The business of tying a lady's girdle round the dragon's neck, leading it captive through the town, and then slaying it amid the town's rejoicing is grotesque and almost repulsive; dragons cannot be dealt with in such stage show—they break loose. But in essential outline the story rightly tells the plight and rescue of mankind.

Jesus' contemporaries believed in a kingdom of evil ruled over by Beliar, the prince of devils.[31] That dread invisible hierarchy caused all sickness and misfortune, a guess that has some merit in a world where nature breeds disease as well as health; and, they said, deliverance would come only with the Messiah. He would grapple with Beliar in the Armageddon of men's souls, and only through Him could victory bless our benighted earth. Is there an eschatological stress throughout the Prayer? Assuredly there is in the petition "Hallowed be thy name," and in "Thy kingdom come." Perhaps the "day by day" of the prayer for bread is an interim prayer that has in mind the imminent Day of the Lord. Perhaps "Deliver us from evil" is really a prayer for the coming of the Deliverer. So only Christ could teach the Prayer. He is God's "best name." In Him the Kingdom comes. By Him the will is done. He is the Bread of life. Only through Him is mankind delivered from evil. There was no romantic touch or triumphal procession when He grappled with the dragon—only a bleak hill and a bleaker cross. But there Beliar was slain: present history in its convulsions is but his death throes. So Jesus taught us to pray "Deliver us from the evil [one]," and Jesus Himself answered the prayer.

V

In many ways God delivers us when we pray. He saves us by strange turn of event; our word "coincidence" is a poor disguise for a Mystery of providence. He saves us by sudden insight which comes, not without prior thought on our part, yet with a newness that can be ascribed only to some primal Source. He saves us through our resolve not to fail those who trust us, and by the demands of our daily work, and by the solace of our homes. But these deliverances would be only temporary reprieves but for Christ; He commutes the sentence of death into the foretaste of eternal life.

There is deliverance, or Jesus would not have taught us to pray for it. The helplessness of man is not merely weakness but the sign royal in our life: we are meant to live by the power of God. But woe to the man who thinks he can work his own deliverance:

> Chaos, Cosmos! Cosmos, Chaos! once again the
> sickening game;

> Freedom, free to slay herself, and dying while
> they shout her name.[32]

And woe to the man who trifles with evil, or deems it a trifle; he walks into a dragon's den. But blessed is the man who knows his helplessness, and cries out on God; his weakness is then his strength: "Power is made perfect in weakness." [33] And blessed is the man who looks for the Deliverer who has broken the power of the father of lies. For that man daily prays the prayer in straits of soul and is daily granted reinforcement and liberty: "Lead us not into temptation, but deliver us from evil."

CHAPTER XVI

The Doxology of the Prayer

"For thine is the kingdom, and the power, and the glory, for ever. Amen."   Matthew 6:13

THIS ASCRIPTION was almost certainly not part of the original prayer. It is not found even in the best manuscripts of the Gospel of Matthew. But it must have come into early use in the Church, for the Didache, a manual of Christian worship and practice written early in the second century, includes it and prescribes its use.[1] Some of the later manuscripts of Matthew's Gospel incorporate it, thus giving further evidence that the Lord's Prayer as we now have it was a liturgy. Some commentators have looked askance at this doxology, claiming that it tends "to turn a religious reality into a devotional form." [2] But why the demurrer? We cannot hope to have the words of Jesus verbatim; He spoke in Aramaic, a now dead language. Moreover a formless reality would have little meaning for mortal men. Why not say that Matthew's Gospel has *enshrined* religious reality in Christ-given devotional form?

The doxology has Jewish antecedents. The Seventy-second Psalm has a similar conclusion: "And blessed be his glorious name for ever: and let the whole earth be filled with his glory; Amen, and Amen." [3] The prayer offered by David at the building of the Temple likewise provides a precedent: "Thine, O Lord, is the greatness, and the power, and the glory, and the victory, and the majesty." [4] Apparently it was a Jewish custom at synagogue services for the people to respond to the prayers with "Amen," but at temple services the response was in longer form: "Blessed be the name of the glory of his kingdom forever." [5] But the Lord's Prayer gives old doxologies an abundant new life. Jesus has a better gift than any Dvořak for turning traditional music into a New World Symphony. True instinct added the doxology, for the Prayer begins with God in the heaven of His purity and love, and the doxology gives it back to the "One God and Father of all, who is above all, and through all, and in you all." [6] Whenever we pray "For thine is the kingdom, and the power, and the glory," the river of human praise returns to the Sea.

I

It is a breath-taking affair that such a doxology should be added to a prayer taught by a Galilean craftsman. Treasure waits beneath that fact, far richer treasure than waits beneath a man at work on the roof of the Metropolitan Museum of Art. Why *should* an ascription of praise to God be added by a persecuted church to a craftsman's prayer? He had taught His handful of disciples that they were to pray to God as their kind and holy Father, that

222

they were to be intent first on His kingdom, that they were to ask in simple faith for bread of body and forgiveness of sins. It was not a new prayer, except in stress and proportion, except as He Himself made it new. Soon He died. His death was so shameful—on a gallows that Jews had long reckoned accursed—that it would almost have been better had He simply disappeared. He was betrayed by one of His disciples, deserted by His friends, and killed under a curse by His foes. So He died. No trumpets sounded on Calvary. The best that could have been said of Him then, at least in mortal reckoning, was what African natives said to Livingstone about the Zambezi River: it "by sand is covered." [7]

But at the turn of the first century the Christian Church, persecuted, composed in part of slaves, added a trumpet burst of praise to His prayer: "For thine is the kingdom, and the power, and the glory." Beneath that fact is treasure and mystery. Men covet what they call "sure proof" of Christ's resurrection. What is sure proof? If they had an affidavit from witnesses, who could prove its genuineness? If some radio skill could pick up His very voice after death, men would still doubt, for they would not know His Aramaic tongue. Perhaps they would be right to doubt; scribblings and sounds are not the proof of Christ. But there is no doubt that a church was raised on the grave of a Man done to shameful death. There is no doubt that they were sure that He was alive after death. There is no doubt that they were quite ready to die in that faith. There is no doubt that they were honest folk,

223

and that had you been looking for simple truth and kindly honor in the world of that day, you would have found it soonest and best in the Church of Christ.

This doxology is therefore for witness that the River disappearing into the sand came back into the sun. How else can the Church be explained, or a doxology at the end of the Prayer He taught? If Matthew's Gospel was written in Syria, and if this doxology was added at the beginning of the second century, we know what conditions encompassed the praise. Christians were persecuted as heretics by the synagogue, denied the privileges of citizenship, boycotted in the market place, and in many instances done to death by the same empire that killed their Lord. Yet when they prayed the Prayer He had taught them, they added an ascription that is like celestial trumpets. They cried out on God in praise: "For thine is the kingdom, and the power, and the glory." Eyes can hardly check tears of joy at this wonder. These early Christians had found in Him, crucified and risen, a joy wealthier than a thousand market places and well worth the cost of ten thousand persecutions. That the Church is unworthy who could doubt? It is bedraggled in its timidities; it is shamed by its outright betrayals. But that fact only makes the vitality of the Church more strange. The Roman Catholic Church, tied too closely to feudalism, lived nevertheless when feudalism passed. The Greek Orthodox Church, tied too closely to czarism, survived when czarism failed and will survive any Soviet sacrilege. The German Lutheran Church, too acquiescent in the rise of

Hitler, lived when Nazism perished in a holocaust. Why does the Church live despite all failure? Not because the Lord is dead! Through Him an old doxology became glad thunder of Easter trumpets: "For thine is the kingdom, and the power, and the glory, for ever. Amen."

II

Jesus gave a new meaning to the word kingdom. The Church knew that in Him the kingdom had come upon them. At Calvary it had been proved stronger than sin. On Easter Day it rose stronger than death. The accent in the doxology is on the word "is"—not as much as on "Thine," and perhaps not as much as on the subsequent nouns, but with glad stress to announce present fact. The rise of any earthly empire is but the early proclamation of its fall. The Roman Empire, apparently invincible, drove a mailed fist through the early church; but the fist withered while the Church lived. All man's systems are doomed—the short span of our generation has seen the decline of the British Empire, and the meteoric rise and fall of the Reich. If this is "the American century," nothing is more sure than that the century will pass. If Soviet Russia comes to world power, that very power is the prophecy of its death.

> Earth might be fair and all men glad and wise.
> Age after age their tragic empires rise,
> Built while they dream, and in that dreaming weep:
> Would man but wake from out his haunted sleep,
> Earth might be fair and all men glad and wise.[8]

The feverish "dream" is that the earth is man's to have and to hold. Men "weep" because that blasphemy brings war with all its sorrows. All man's empires are "tragic empires."

Alice Meynell has an essay,[9] characteristic of her gentleness and strong sense of reality, in which she describes how grass and flowers invade the city of Rome. There is a tuft, she says, on every lofty cornice; and flowers grow on each high ecclesiastical ledge. Perhaps it is true that "man made the city, but God made the country"; for the country, seemingly weak, proves at last far stronger than the city. Man's stone cities cannot stay the invasion even of meadow grass. Fields shall wave, or deserts spread their calcined death, where tanks now roll in military might through proud streets. "For thine is the kingdom." Man's kingdoms care little for the man living on Main Street, and less for the child, for to an empire any individual is but a wisp of cannon fodder. But the invisible Kingdom counts each one of them precious; "not one of them will fall," [10] because the kingdom is a Father's kingdom. This the Church knew, and knows, through Christ. Therefore the Church bows in homage, with grateful heart, before the only kingdom—the Kingdom that was, and is, and evermore shall be.

III

Jesus gave new meaning to the word power. Our generation has discovered power. But it has claimed it for its own, in the futile attempt of the creature to become his own god. It has forgotten that the power belongs to God, and that it becomes suicidal when used contrary to His will. Look closely at the psychology induced by an aircraft carrier. It provokes the nation owning it to say, "Now I can defend myself." Yet it spreads fear lest other nations should build a larger carrier. Meanwhile there is always at the back of the owner's mind an awareness that man the creature cannot long defend himself. Meanwhile the carrier provokes other nations to say, "That carrier threatens me, so I must build a larger carrier." Mixed with this feeling of threat is injured pride. Then begins an armament race. Meanwhile some general in the one land says: "We must build a larger carrier so that we may be secure." It rarely occurs to him that some general in the other land says precisely the same thing. The race has gone far, all the way from bows and arrows to H-bombs. When a war occurs between two powerful rivals, a third power says of the victor: "We may be the next to be conquered; we must take advantage of his temporary exhaustion to build our national security." Thus power induces madness whenever power is turned from God's purposes to the fancied good of the creature.

Power as men conceive it is an affair of the body; but man is soul-in-body, and the only real power is that which girds the soul. Therefore the description of the power of Christ: "But as many as received him, to them gave he power to become the sons of God." [11] Power as men conceive it is an affair of time, but man is child of both time and eternity; and he dimly knows that time is marked out for destruction, and that his real life is in an eternal realm. Therefore the description of the power of Christ: "power over all flesh, that he should give eternal life to as many as thou hast given him." [12] The body is soon spent: why should a man waste his life on body power when soul power is his for the asking? Time flies: why should a man toss his life away on time power when eternal power beckons him in love? Hate is a carcinoma: why should a man curse himself with the power of hate when by God's gift he may live "after the power of an endless life"?[13] Man's power is a fake. Let the reader underline the word power in the columns of today's newspaper; he will find that in almost every instance it is the mask of death. Then let him underline the word power in the Bible; he will find that in every instance, except those that describe the cankered and transitory power of evil, it is the promise of life. Carlyle contrasts the guns and guillotine of the French Revolution with the Sacrament of the Lord's Table.[14] There is only one revolution—the salvation of the soul. There is only one power—the power of God's love made known in His incarnate Son.

IV

Jesus gave new meaning to the word glory. What a shabby, death-shrouded word it has become in man's dictionaries! Thomas Gray has the truth: "The paths of glory lead but to the grave." [15] When a new pope is consecrated, the choir intones: *"Sic transit gloria mundi"*: "Swiftly passes the glory of this world." Yet men still grasp at glory, and it still eludes them. Not even popes have refused the sorry scramble, despite the intoned warning. Try "glory" as a word test on your friends. Ask them what it means to them. Many will think instantly of a royal procession or a presidential train; perhaps even of lights on Broadway, or a celebrity pursued by autograph hunters. A few may recall the splendor of sunrise or sunset. Still fewer may remember that Francis of Assisi tore down in anger the tiles of the shrine men proposed to build in his honor. Is Francis more "glorious" than the proud Bishop Ugolimo who tried to regiment the Franciscan Order for the "good" of the Church? [16] Still fewer, a mere handful, will think of Christ dying on a cross.

One of the most astonishing stories in the Old Testament tells how Moses asked that he might see God's glory. The answer came: "I will make all my goodness pass before thee." [17] Is not the goodness of God the truest glory of God? Suns and stars are His glory, and mountains that cleave the sky. Perchance in other worlds there are sunrises that make ours seem dullness, and hosts of winged seraphim chanting round a Throne. But these glories would not be glorious if God were not good; they would be but pride and terror. The root of the word glory is light, the French *gloire*. When Jesus rose from the dead, He did not wither Caiaphas in the Temple or Pilate in his palace, or unfurl the banners of heaven to confound his foes. He overtook two obscure disciples on a lonely road to comfort their sad hearts,[18] and appeared to a fear-stricken group meeting behind locked doors.[19]

"Go . . . tell his disciples and Peter" [20]—Peter being the man who had denied that he ever knew his Lord! Thus the stories speak their own essential truth. In Jesus is true glory—the glory of love without which all splendor would only strike death.

V

The doxology to the Lord's Prayer is the redemption of our world. For it is the surrender of man's will in worship. Our needs are few—bread, pardon, and fealty. We need fealty more than we need bread; for unless we have some Loyalty for whom to die, it is not worth our while to live. The ebb of faith during the last century did not kill our need for fealty, for skepticisms do not easily change our elemental hungers. Fealty to God being temporarily thwarted, the hunger to worship still remained —and Hitler rushed in to fill the vacuum. When men spurn noble religion, they do not become irreligious, for it is not possible for man to alter the constitution of the soul. No, when noble religion is spurned, a cheap religion takes its place—some worship of the state, some adulation of a fellow mortal. Then when the new god has led the race into the quagmire, men see that they have followed "wandering fires." Only the worship of God can save us from that desolation. As often as men say with sincerity, "Thine is the kingdom," they are saved from a debasing self-worship, and by the same token they are united in primal Loyalty.

It is a sorry portent that banks, office buildings, and

universities now tower above churches. In the Middle Ages the cities were not as sanitary as ours, and not as proud, but the cathedral rose above them. Rich and poor together helped to build the shrine, and brought their gifts. Thus they testified that earth is tragic unless dedicate to a Will above the earth. Science can bless us only as it is first dedicate. Learning will be at best a transitory pride of mind, and at worst a devising of more wholesale slaughter, unless it is held in reverence. Trade will become a dusty death, until it is given in homage. All talk of science, learning, and trade is still talk about ourselves; and we ourselves are only frail creatures of time, bereft whenever we deny the Life beyond our life. The only motto for a new age is "Thine is the kingdom, and the power, and the glory." Men are tall only when they kneel. Men are truly one family only when they pray.

VI

The Lord's Prayer, as it has come to us in the magnificent liturgy of Matthew, ends in "Amen." That is a massive word fallen by our neglect upon evil days. To many people it is only the welcome sign that the weariness of public worship has ended. Worship rightly offered is not a weariness; it is earth's highest art and awe-struck joy. "Amen" is the word Jesus used when He wished to stress a truth, the word translated in our Bibles "Verily": "Amen, Amen, I say to you." It is the word used by pious Jews in Jesus' day when they responded to the synagogue prayers. It means "So let it be!" It is an act of final faith:

God will bring it to pass. It is the glad surrender of the soul: I offer myself to God so that He may bring it to pass through me, if He so please.

The old song about an organist who half unaware struck the chords of a "great amen," [21] and then could not recover it, is true to life. The proposal of the song, that such an Amen will be found again "only in heaven," is not bathos. Every man is Abt Vogler;[22] he catches strains of music that ever afterward elude him, at least this side of death. Struggling churches in Syria, when Matthew lived and wrote, prayed the Prayer and concluded it with a "great Amen": "Thine is the kingdom, and the power, and the glory. Amen." But the kingdom of Rome still harried them, the power of death encompassed them, and the false glory of man mocked their faith. Was their "Amen" therefore lost? No, for "there shall never be one lost good":[23]

The high that proved too high, the heroic for earth too hard,
The passion that left the ground to lose itself in the sky,
Are music sent up to God by the lover and the bard;
Enough that he heard it once: we shall hear it by and by.[23]

The Lord's Prayer is too vast for earth and far too radiant; therefore it is a foretaste and prophecy of heaven. That we may pray it at all stamps us with the seal of an eternal Land, where we shall know that God has always ruled in love: "For thine is the kingdom, and the power, and the glory for ever. Amen."

References

I. Born to Believe

1. I Corinthians 13:1, using "love" instead of "charity."
2. Symposium "Religion and the Intellectuals," *Partisan Review*, Vol. XVII, No. 2 (February, 1950), p. 116.
3. *New Lights on the Old Faith*, p. 60, as quoted in *The Great Texts of the Bible*, ed. James Hastings (New York: Charles Scribner's Sons, 1914), XVIII (Thess. to Heb.), 190.
4. *Barabbas the Robber*, produced by J. Arthur Rank, distributed through United World Films, Inc.
5. Symposium "Religion and the Intellectuals," pp. 134-35.
6. William Garden Blaikie, *David Brown, D.D., LLD.*, p. 147, as quoted in *The Great Texts of the Bible, loc. cit.*
7. Thomas C. Upham, *Life and Religious Opinions and Experience of Madame de la Mothe Guyon* (New York: Harper & Bros., 1871) II, 376.

II. Faith in God

1. *The Works of William Paley* (Boston: Joshua Belcher, 1810), Vol. I, *Natural Theology*, chap. 1.
2. (New York: The Macmillan Co., 1919), esp. Part I, chap. 6.
3. Acts 17:28.
4. See *Look*, September 19, 1944, p. 6. The letter quoted was written in reply to an article entitled "Religion in the Front Lines," in the issue of July 25, 1944, p. 48.
5. Letter to *The Bookman*, Vol. V, No. 1 (March 1897), p. 7, referring to a notice of his book of poems *The Torrent and the Night Before* (New York: Dodd, Mead & Co., 1897).
6. Cf. George Bernard Shaw, *The Doctor's Dilemma*, Act V, where Dr. Ridgeon says: "The soul is an organ I have not come across in the course of my anatomical work."

7. Tennyson, "The Ancient Sage," 1. 49.

8. Tennyson, "The Higher Pantheism," st. 6.

9. See F. Barrows Colton, "Mapping the Unknown Universe," *National Geographic,* September, 1950, pp. 401-2; also Sir James Jeans, *The Universe Around Us* (New York: The Macmillan Co., 1929), pp. 35, 61, 66-68, 81-85, 256-57; and James H. Jeans, *The Stars in Their Courses* (New York: The Macmillan Co., 1931), pp. 85, 136. The illustration of the train is a simple mater of calculation.

10. Wordsworth, "Tintern Abbey," 1. 97.

11. *Faith and Society* (New York: Longmans, Green & Co., 1932) p. 111.

12. Thomas Moore, "Where Is Your Dwelling, Ye Sainted?" st. 2.

13. George Santayana, "O World, Thou Choosest Not," *Poems* (New York: Charles Scribner's Sons, 1923), Sonnet iii.

14. Philippians 2:8.

15. Amy Lowell, *John Keats* (Boston: Houghton Mifflin Co., 1925), I, 94, 193.

16. John 1:14 (R.S.V.).

17. *The Problem of Pain* (New York: The Macmillan Co. 1947). See esp. pp. 1-2, 12-13, but the argument runs throughout.

18. Irving S. Cobb (New York: George H. Doran Co., 1915).

19. Thomas Hood, "The Bridge of Sighs," st. 9.

20. Francis Thompson, "The Hound of Heaven," 1. 154.

21. *The Works of Walter Bagehot,* ed. Forrest Morgan (Hartford: Travelers Insurance Co., 1880), I, 179, in his essay "Mr. Clough's Poems."

22. A concordance gives many references for this phrase, e.g. Job 28:28; Proverbs 23:17; Isaiah 2:19, 21.

23. Romans 11:33.

24. *The Testament of Beauty* (New York: Oxford University Press, 1930), 1. 350.

25. "The Prayer of Miriam Cohen," *Rudyard Kipling's Verse* (Garden City: Doubleday, Doran & Co., 1945), st. 3.

26. Hosea 6:3.

27. From "Truth," *The Canterbury Tales,* tr. Frank Ernest Hill (New York: Longmans, Green & Co., 1930), p. 188.
28. II Corinthians 5:1.

III. *Faith in Jesus Christ*

1. Quoted from memory. A careful search has failed to discover the source; however, I believe it is accurate.
2. John Morley, *Rousseau* (London: Chapman & Hall, 1873), "Preliminary," p. 4. Lord Morley originally had "divine" instead of "sublime"—see F. W. Hirst, *Early Life and Letters of John Morley* (London: Macmillan & Co., 1927), I, 222.
3. Cf. Genesis 2:23.
4. Matthew 27:11; Mark 15:2; Luke 23:3.
5. D. S. Merejkowski, *Jesus the Unknown,* tr. H. Chrouschoff Matheson (New York: Charles Scribner's Sons, 1934); Giovanni Papini, *Life of Christ,* tr. Dorothy Canfield Fisher (New York: Harcourt, Brace & Co., 1923); William Ellery Leonard, *The Poet of Galilee* (New York: Viking Press, 1928); Conrad Noel, *The Life of Jesus* (New York: Simon & Schuster, 1937); Maurice Goguel, *The Life of Jesus* (New York: The Macmillan Co., 1933).
6. Daniel Johnson Fleming (New York: Friendship Press, 1938). The statue mentioned is "The Christ of the Andes" by the Argentine sculptor Mateo Alonso, dedicated March, 1904, to commemorate peace between Argentina and Chile.
7. Luke 23:4.
8. II Timothy 2:8.
9. *The Republic,* Bk. 7, chap 1.
10. Ephesians 4:15.
11. Written by an unknown German writer of the seventeenth century, tr. R. Storrs Willis c. 1850, st. 2.
12. Philippians 2:8.
13. Nicene Creed.
14. Hosea 6:3.

IV. *Faith in the Holy Spirit*

1. Mark 15:39; Luke 23:46; John 19:30.
2. Milton, *Paradise Lost*, Bk. 11, 1. 995.
3. Acts 2.
4. I Corinthians 14:19 (R.S.V.).
5. Edward Gibbon, *The Decline and Fall of the Roman Empire*, chap. 23.
6. Acts 2:2, 3.
7. *The Scarlet Letter*, chap. XI.
8. Browning, "Christmas Eve," canto VII.
9. Judges 6:11 (my translation).
10. Acts 19:2 (R.S.V.).
11. John 16:12 (R.S.V.).
12. John 16:13, 15.
13. Matthew 11:19.
14. In 1924.
15. Francis Turner Palgrave, "Thou Say'st, 'Take Up Thy Cross,'" st. 2.
16. John 16:7.
17. John 14:16, 17.
18. Luke 24:13-35.
19. John 16:14.
20. John 16:8 (R.S.V.).
21. Palgrave, *op. cit.*, st. 7.
22. I John 2:1.
23. Edwin Hatch, 1886, st. 1.
24. R. A. Streatfeild, *Handel* (New York: John Lane Co., 1909), p. 219.
25. Matthew 10:19.
26. Ernest Raymond, *In the Steps of St. Francis* (New York: H. C. Kinsey & Co., Inc., 1939), pp. 223-25.
27. Acts 1:8 (R.S.V.).
28. Genesis 11:1-9.
29. *The Doctrine of the Trinity* (New York: Charles Scribner's Sons, 1944), esp. Lecture 7.
30. *"Veni, Creator Spiritus,"* tr. Bishop John Cosin, 1627.

REFERENCES

31. Acts 1:4.
32. John 16:13.
33. Joel 2:28.
34. Quoted in Adam W. Burnett, *The Lord Reigneth* (London: Hodder & Stoughton, 1946), p. 78.

V. *Faith in the Church*

1. Hebrews 12:23.
2. *The Works of Robert G. Ingersoll* (New York: The Ingersoll Publishers, Inc., 1900), I (Lectures), 466.
3. John 17:21 (R.S.V.).
4. John 10:16.
5. An event well known in England. See Gordon Hurlbutt, *Windows and Wings* (Louisville: Standard Press, 1928), p. 221.
6. Matthew 6:6.
7. Matthew 18:20.
8. A phrase, I think, from St. Ambrose.
9. See Hurlbutt, *op. cit.*, p. 61.
10. Lloyd C. Douglas (Chicago: Willett, Clark & Co., 1929).
11. Shakespeare, *The Merchant of Venice*, Act IV, scene 1.
12. Matthew 6:3.
13. "I Heard the Voice of Jesus Say," H. Bonar, 1846, st. 3.
14. Philippians 4:22.
15. Depicts the Battle of Atlanta, July 22, 1864, painted by three German artists, Lohr, Lorenz, and Heine. This particular episode is described by Hurlbutt, *op. cit.*, p. 159.
16. Tennyson, *In Memoriam*, prologue, st. 5.
17. R. R. Madden, M.R.I.A., *The Life and Martyrdom of Savonarola* (London: Thomas C. Newby, 1854), II, 101-2.
18. "The Church's One Foundation," S. J. Stone, 1866, st. 4.
19. Proverbs 27:6.
20. Psalm 46:4.

VI. *Faith in Forgiveness*

1. Victor Hugo, *Les Miserables*, tr. Charles E. Wilbour, "Fantine," Bk. 2, chaps. 6, 10-12.

2. John 9:41 (R.S.V.).
3. Shakespeare.
4. Feodor Mikhailovich Dostoyevsky, tr. Constance Garnett.
5. Tennyson, "Sea Dreams," l. 168.
6. Abe Martin was the brain child of Frank McKinney Hubbard (Kin Hubbard), humorist and caricaturist. The "Abe Martin" cartoons appeared regularly in the *Indianapolis News* and have since been collected in such books as *Abe Martin's Primer* and *Abe Martin's Almanac*.
7. Matthew 5:44; Luke 6:27, 28.
8. John S. C. Abbott, *The History of Napoleon Bonaparte* (New York: Harper & Bros., 1855), II, 141.
9. Matthew 9:2; Mark 2:3; Luke 6:20.
10. See Albert Schweitzer, *Out of My Life and Thought,* tr. C. T. Campion (New York: Henry Holt & Co., 1933).
11. "There Is a Green Hill Far Away," C. F. Alexander, 1848, st. 2.
12. Lamentations 1:12. See also Handel, *The Messiah*.
13. See Shakespeare, *King Lear*.
14. John 2:29.
15. Luke 23:34.
16. II Corinthians 5:21 (R.S.V.).
17. Quoted in H. L. Mencken, *A New Dictionary of Quotations* (New York: Alfred A. Knoff, 1942), p. 418.
18. Thomas Carlyle, *History of Friedrich the Second* (New York: Harper & Bros., 1858), Bk. X, chap. VIII.
19. Luke 18:10-14.
20. I John 4:19.
21. Ephesians 4:32.

VII. *Faith in Life Eternal*

1. I Corinthians 15:56.
2. Acts 16:30.
3. *The Right to Believe* (New York: Charles Scribner's Sons, 1938), pp. 82-84.
4. Shakespeare, *Hamlet*, Act II, scene 2.

REFERENCES

5. *Ibid.*, Act III, scene 1.
6. Traditional. A well-known setting is by Percy Grainger.
7. I Corinthians 15:26.
8. From the Apostles' Creed.
9. A. Smellie, *In the Secret Place*, p. 377, as quoted in *The Great Texts of the Bible*, XII (John 13–21), 77.
10. II Timothy 1:10.
11. Mark 12:18, 24.
12. Luke 12:4 (R.S.V.).
13. Thompson, "The Hound of Heaven," l. 145.
14. I Corinthians 3:18.
15. See Maurice Goguel, *Jesus the Nazarene, Myth or History*, tr. Frederick Stephens (New York: D. Appleton & Co., 1926), chap. 1.
16. Romans 9:1.
17. I Corinthians 15:14, 15.
18. I Corinthians 15:5, 6.
19. Mark 16:7.
20. Luke 24:15.
21. Matthew 28:9.
22. John 20:21.
23. Tennyson, "Crossing the Bar," st. 3.
24. Luke 24:21.
25. Handel, *The Messiah*.
26. From the Apostles' Creed.
27. II Timothy 1:10.
28. *The History and Life of the Rev. John Tauler of Strasburg*, tr. Susanna Winkworth (London: H. R. Allenson, n.d.).
29. Revelation 21:21.
30. Revelation 14:2.
31. Revelation 15:2.
32. Revelation 22:25.
33. Ephesians 3:19.
34. Hebrews 7:16.
35. Jude 21.
36. See Chap. II, reference 8.

37. The statue of the Christ, surrounded by the twelve apostles, is in the Frue Kirk in Copenhagen. See Eugene Plon, *Thorvaldsen: His Life and Works* (Boston: Roberts Bros., 1873), pp. 90, 219-20. This story of the child is told by Edgar DeWitt Jones, and is quoted in *Treasury of the Christian Faith*, ed. Stanley I. Stuber and Thomas Curtis Clark (New York: Association Press, 1949), p. 377.

VIII. *The Lord's Prayer and Our Prayers*

1. Abbott, *op. cit.*, I, 169-70.
2. Luke 11:1.
3. The Shema (Shemoneh Esreh) or Eighteen Benedictions. See W. O. E. Oesterley, *The Jewish Background of the Christian Liturgy* (Oxford: Clarendon Press, 1925), pp. 42 ff., 59 ff.
4. Matthew 6:7.
5. Acts 19:34.
6. Harrison Forman, *Through Forbidden Tibet* (New York: Longmans, Green & Co., 1935), pp. 22-29, and Index.
7. Herman Melville.
8. Matthew 5:17.
9. See Oesterley, *op. cit.*, pp. 151 ff., who shows how far the Lord's Prayer might be influenced by synagogal liturgy.
10. See Canon F. W. Green, *The Gospel According to Saint Matthew*, "The Clarendon Bible" (Oxford: Clarendon Press, 1945), p. 140.
11. Lowell, "The Present Crisis."
12. Quoted in *Treasury of the Christian Faith*, p. 512.
13. J. D. Jones, *The Model Prayer* (New York: George H. Doran Co., 1899).
14. Cf. J. D. Jones, *op cit.*, p. 92, who attributes to C. H. Spurgeon what appears a variant of the same story.
15. Dante, *The Divine Comedy*, "Paradiso," Canto III, l. 85.
16. See Matthew 7: 7-8; 21:21.
17. Psalm 118:23.
18. Matthew 28:18.

REFERENCES

IX. *Our Father*

1. Matthew 6:9.
2. Luke 11:2.
3. Luke 11:1.
4. Psalm 103:13.
5. Robert Browning, "Rabbi Ben Ezra."
6. In 1924.
7. See Chap. VIII, reference 15.
8. Fitzgerald, *The Rubáiyát of Omar Khayyám* (1st ed.), st. lii.
9. Job 15:15.
10. Leviticus 11:44.
11. *The Rubáiyát of Omar Khayyám* (1st ed.), sts. lx, lxi, lxiv.
12. Matthew 10:27.
13. *In Memoriam.*
14. Marjorie Hillis (Indianapolis: Bobbs-Merrill Co., 1936).
15. A phrase of Josiah Royce, *The Problem of Christianity* (New York: The Macmillan Co., 1913). Vol. I, pp. xxv, 172; also see Index.
16. *A Christmas Carol.*
17. Matthew Henry, *An Exposition of the Old and New Testaments* (1708-10), on Ps. 23:6. Used as title of a novel by Rachel Lyman Field (New York: The Macmillan Co., 1938).
18. See D. C. Somervell, *A Short History of Our Religion* (London: George Bell & Sons, Ltd., 1936), p. 47.
19. *Titian*, tr. Charles T. Brooks (Boston: Ticknor & Fields, 1863), Vol. II, Cycle 145.
20. Isaiah 40:31.
21. II Corinthians 5:19.
22. Charles Dejob, *Marc Antoine Muret* (Paris: Ernest Thorin, 1881), p. 60. Donald H. Tippett, *The Desires of a Religious Man* (New York: Fleming H. Revell Co., 1942), pp. 40-41, refers to the same story, using the Latinized form of Muret's name. Muret was an outstanding Latin scholar of his age.

X. *The Hallowed Name*

1. *The Creed of Christ* (New York: Harper & Bros., 1940), p. 45.
2. Isaiah 6:3.
3. From John Bunyan, *The Holy War or, the Losing and Taking of the Town of Mansoul* (1682).
4. Deuteronomy 5:11.
5. John 15:16.
6. Galatians 4:6.
7. John 14:9.
8. (New York: Fleming H. Revell Co., 1942), pp. 22-27.
9. (New York and Nashville: Abingdon-Cokesbury Press, 1942), pp. 32-35.
10. *Op. cit.*, p. 45.
11. James Elmes, *Memoirs of the Life and Works of Sir Christopher Wren* (London: Priestley & Weale, 1823), pp. 475-76. Dr. Macartney, *op. cit.*, 27, makes fuller reference to this.
12. Isaiah 6:3.

XI. *The Coming of the Kingdom*

1. "An American," *Rudyard Kipling's Verse*, st. 6.
2. Psalm 145:13.
3. Lowell, "The Vision of Sir Launfal," Part I, Prelude.
4. Thompson, "The Hound of Heaven," 1. 143.
5. Hebrews 10:31.
6. I remember reading this in a newspaper or magazine but have been unable to rediscover the item.
7. See Chap. X, reference 3.
8. Luke 18:13. I have used "the" instead of "a" to accord with the force of the Greek.
9. *Studies in the Lord's Prayer*, p. 29, as quoted in *The Great Texts of the Bible*, VIII (Matt.), 141-42.
10. *Op. cit.*, pp. 83-84.
11. Luke 4: 25-26; I Kings 17: 9-24.
12. Luke 4:27; II Kings 5.

REFERENCES

13. I am considerably indebted in this section to Canon Green's "special note" on the kingdom, *op cit.*, p. 187, note D.
14. Mark 4:26.29.
15. Luke 17:21.
16. Matthew 4:17. This is my translation based on the translation offered by Sherman E. Johnson in his Exegesis of Matthew written for *The Interpreter's Bible* (New York and Nashville: Abingdon-Cokesbury Press, 1951), VII, 275.
17. Matthew 12:28 (R.S.V.).
18. Psalm 97:11.
19. Viola Meynell, *Alice Meynell; A Memoir* (New York: Charles Scribner's Sons, 1929), p. 143.
20. C. S. Lewis (New York: The Macmillan Co., 1947), p. 13.

XII. *The Will of God*

1. See Canon Green, *op. cit.*, pp. 140, 141; Arthur S. Peake, ed., *A Commentary on the Bible* (London: T. C. & E. C. Jack, Ltd., 1920), p. 706*b*.
2. Matthew 26:42.
3. Luke 22:53.
4. John 18:1.
5. *The Rubáiyát of Omar Khayyám* (5th ed.), st. lxix.
6. Percy MacKaye, "Goethals." This poem was recited by its author at the National Testimonial to Colonel George W. Goethals, March 4, 1914.
7. Longfellow, "The Light of the Stars," st. 7.
8. *Romeo and Juliet*, Act V, scene 1, l. 75.
9. Thompson, "The Hound of Heaven," l. 19.
10. Milton, "Sonnet on His Blindness."
11. Shakespeare, *Hamlet*, Act V, scene 2, l. 11.
12. Psalm 24:1.
13. *In Memoriam*, introduction, st. 4.
14. Philippians 2:9.
15. See Chap. VIII, reference 15.
16. James Culross, *William Carey* (London: Hodder & Stough-

ton, 1881), p. 43.

17. John 4:34.
18. Matthew 26:42.
19. John 5:6.
20. *The Pilgrim's Progress,* Part I.
21. Seymour Van Santvoord, "Canticle of the Sun," *Saint Francis* (New York: E. P. Dutton & Co., 1927), p. 72.
22. Philippians 2:12-13.
23. Colossians 4:12.

XIII. *God and Our Daily Bread*

1. This papyrus published by Sayce in W. M. Flinders Petrie, *Hawara, Biahmu and Arsinoe* (London, 1889), is described by Sherman Johnson, *op. cit.,* VII, 313.
2. *Op. cit.,* chap. IV.
3. H. Robertson Nicholl, ed., *The Expositor's Greek Testament* (New York: George H. Doran Co., n.d.), I, 121; and Frederic Henry Chase, *The Lord's Prayer in the Early Church, Texts and Studies,* ed. J. Armitage Robinson (Cambridge: University Press, 1891), pp. 49, 52-53.
4. Matthew 25:31-46.
5. Frederic W. H. Myers, *Saint Paul* (London: Macmillan & Co., 1910), p. 15.
6. Maltbie D. Babcock, "Give Us This Day Our Daily Bread," *Thoughts for Every-Day Living* (New York: Charles Scribner's Sons, 1901), p. 167.
7. The Iona Community in Scotland. See G. F. MacLeod, *We Shall Rebuild* (Philadelphia: Kirkridge, 1945), esp. p. 83.
8. Chap. 4.
9. Maarten Maartens (pseud.), *My Lady Nobody* (New York: Harper & Bros., 1895), p. 8.
10. Matthew 6:26 (R.S.V.).
11. *Letters of James Smetham,* ed. Sarah Smetham and William Davies (New York: Macmillan & Co., 1891), p. 231—in a letter to C. M. written in 1871.

12. *Journals,* ed. Waldo Emerson Forbes (Boston: Houghton Mifflin Co., 1909-14), V, 406, entry for May 30, 1840.

13. Luke 12:15.

14. Rackham Holt, *George Washington Carver* (New York: Doubleday, Doran & Co., 1943), pp. 181 ff.

15. Archibald MacLeish, *Panic* (Boston: Houghton Mifflin Co., 1935), p. 18.

16. Luke 24:30 (R.S.V.).

17. See William Manson, *The Gospel of Luke,* "The Moffatt New Testament Commentary" (New York: Harper & Bros., 1930), p. 135.

18. Matthew 4:4.

19. "The Sovereignty of Ethics," *Lectures and Biographical Sketches* (Boston: Houghton Mifflin Co., 1887), p. 202.

20. This is Marcion's translation. See *The Abingdon Bible Commentary* (New York: Abingdon Press, 1929), p. 966a.

21. The Rev. E. S. Buchanan, in a lecture given at Union Theological Seminary, New York, December 8, 1914. See *The Expositor,* X (1915), 423. This version in Latin was actually written underneath the traditional form.

22. I Corinthians 11:24.

23. Proverbs 4:18.

XIV. *The Prayer for Pardon*

1. The first English Bible translated from the original tongues, printed in Worms in 1525 by Peter Schoeffer. See Sir Frederic Kenyon, *Our Bible and the Ancient Manuscripts* (New York: Harper & Bros., 1940), pp. 212-17. The manuscript is in the British Museum.

2. Joe McCarthy, quoted from memory.

3. Philippians 3:14.

4. I Timothy 1:15.

5. I read this confession in an unpublished manuscript, and I am quoting from reading memory.

6. *Book of American Negro Spirituals,* ed. J. W. Johnson (New York: Viking Press, 1940) , Part 2, p. 136.
7. Tennyson, "Maud," Part X, st. 6.
8. Shakespeare, *Macbeth,* Act V, scene iii, l. 46.
9. *Op. cit.,* p. 115.
10. Act IV, scene 2.
11. Romans 5:8.
12. Galatians 2:20.
13. Ephesians 2:8.
14. Romans 3:4, 6.
15. Luke 11:4—my translation.
16. Chase, *op. cit.,* p. 56.
17. *Op. cit.,* p. 135.
18. W. H. Wilkins, *Caroline the Illustrious* (London and New York: Longmans, Green & Co., 1901) , II, p. 367.
19. Matthew 18:34.
20. "Essay on Criticism," Part II, l. 324.
21. Ephesians 4:32.

XV. *The Prayer for Deliverance from Evil*

1. *Our Translated Gospels* (New York: Harper & Bros., 1936) , p. 15.
2. See Alfred Plummer, *A Critical and Exegetical Commentary on the Gospel According to St. Luke,* "International Critical Commentary" (Edinburgh: T. & T. Clark, 1896) , p. 298.
3. James 1:13.
4. *Op. cit.,* p. 135.
5. Matthew 26:41.
6. *The Philosophy of Kant,* selected and tr. by John Watson, (Glasgow: James Maclehose & Sons, 1908) , p. 225—from "The Metaphysic of Morality."
7. Matthew 4:1.
8. Luke 4:1-2.
9. *Life and Letters of Thomas Henry Huxley,* ed. Leonard Huxley (New York: D. Appleton & Co., 1913) , I, 352-53. A more complete quotation is included by Dr. Tittle, *op. cit.,* p. 109.

REFERENCES

10. Job 5:7.
11. Wordsworth, "Ode on Intimations of Immortality," st. 9.
12. Wordsworth, "Tintern Abbey," l. 37.
13. See description in *The Columbia Encyclopedia*, p. 74.
14. Titus 1:15 (R.S.V.).
15. "Abt Vogler," st. IX.
16. Matthew 4:3, 6 (R.S.V.).
17. Richard Rodgers and Oscar Hammerstein II, "Some Enchanted Evening," *South Pacific* (1949).
18. Ephesians 6:12 (R.S.V.).
19. *Paradise Regained*, Book I, l. 315.
20. Bunyan, *The Pilgrim's Progress*, Part I.
21. Hilaire Belloc, "The False Heart," *Sonnets and Verse* (New York: Sheed & Ward, 1944).
22. Jeremiah 17:9.
23. Matthew 15:19.
24. See Charles M. Gayley, *The Classic Myths* (New York: Ginn & Co., 1911), pp. 307-8.
25. *The Screwtape Letters*, p. 55.
26. Luke 22:53.
27. (New York: Harper & Bros., 1943), p. 19.
28. Augustine, *Confessions*, Bk. 1, sec. 1.
29. Gayley, *op. cit.*, p. 9.
30. Luke 12:49-50.
31. See Chase, *op. cit.*, pp. 87-89.
32. Tennyson, "Locksley Hall Sixty Years After."
33. II Corinthians 12:9 (R.S.V.).

XVI. *The Doxology of the Prayer*

1. Edgar J. Goodspeed, *The Apostolic Fathers* (New York: Harper & Bros., 1950), p. 15.
2. *The Expositor's Greek Testament*, I, 122.
3. Vs. 19.
4. I Chronicles 29:11.
5. See Oesterley, *op. cit.*, pp. 70-71, 77.

6. Ephesians 4:6.
7. Arthur Vine Hall, "At the Victoria Falls," *Poems of a South African;* quoted by R. J. Campbell, *Livingstone* (New York: Dodd, Mead & Co., 1930), forepage.
8. Clifford Bax, "Turn Back, O Man," st. 2.
9. "Ceres' Runaway," *The Essays of Alice Meynell* (New York: Charles Scribner's Sons, 1914), p. 4.
10. Matthew 10:29 (R.S.V.).
11. John 1:12.
12. John 17:2.
13. Hebrews 7:16.
14. *The French Revolution,* Part II, Bk. I, chap. IX.
15. "Elegy in a Country Churchyard," l. 36.
16. Raymond, *op. cit.,* pp. 203-4.
17. Exodus 33:19.
18. Luke 24:13-35.
19. John 20:19-25.
20. Mark 16:7.
21. Adelaide A. Procter, "The Lost Chord."
22. See Robert Browning's poem "Abt Vogler."
23. *Ibid.*

Index

249

INDEX

253

INDEX

255